A Separate Peace
The War Within

TWAYNE'S MASTERWORK STUDIES
Robert Lecker, General Editor

A Separate Peace
THE WAR WITHIN

HALLMAN BELL BRYANT

Twayne Publishers • *Boston*
A Division of G.K. Hall & Co.

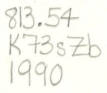

813.54
K73sZb
1990

A Separate Peace: The War Within
Hallman Bell Bryant

Twayne's Masterwork Studies No. 50
Copyright 1990 by G.K. Hall & Co.
All rights reserved.
Published by Twayne Publishers
A division of G.K. Hall & Co.
70 Lincoln Street, Boston, Massachusetts 02111

Copyediting supervised by Barbara Sutton.
Book production by Gabrielle B. McDonald.
Typeset in 10/14 Sabon with Palatino display type by Huron Valley
Graphics, Inc., of Ann Arbor, Michigan.

Printed on permanent/durable acid-free paper
and bound in the United States of America.

Library of Congress Cataloging-in-Publication Data

Bryant, Hallman Bell, 1936–
A separate peace : the war within / Hallman Bell Bryant.
    p.   cm.—(Twayne's masterwork studies ; no. 50)
Includes bibliographical references.
1. Knowles, John, 1926–   Separate peace. I. Title. II. Series.
PS3561.N68S434 1990
813′.54—dc20   89-26817
                                                        CIP

0-8057-8087-4 (alk. paper). 10 9 8 7 6 5 4 3 2 1
0-8057-8131-5 (pbk. alk. paper). 10 9 8 7 6 5 4 3 2 1
First published 1990

Contents

Note on References and Acknowledgments

This study assumes familiarity with the text of *A Separate Peace* and is intended for the reader who desires to understand the larger range of issues that the novel conveys. Like any title that has acquired the status of a masterwork, it has attracted much good critical literature, and I am indebted to numerous commentators on *A Separate Peace* who went before and provided useful exegesis of the novel's many facets. In this booklength study of *A Separate Peace*, I have not attempted a "new reading" of the book so much as an extended reading. All the scholarship to date has been of article length, and thus the range or focus of any given commentary is limited by the critical format. The enlarged scope of the Masterwork Studies series allows for a more comprehensive approach, which I have tried to take, through a consideration of the characteristic elements of the novel. My purpose in this study is to provide practical criticism of the novel through a close analytical and interpretative reading of each chapter in sequence and by a consideration of the basic functional elements—setting, atmosphere, plot action, style, characterization, and theme as emphasized through allegory and symbol.

As Brooks and Warren said in *Understanding Fiction*, ". . . a piece of fiction is a tissue of significances, some great and some small, but all of them aspects, finally, of the total significance of the piece."

Since the standard hardback edition of *A Separate Peace* published by Macmillan is not as widely available as the Dell-Bantam paperback, I have used as reference the paperback edition, which has gone through seventy printings with over 7,445,000 copies now in print. All references are to this edition, which is cited parenthetically throughout the text.

In the process of writing this study I incurred debts to many people whose kindnesses I would like to repay by the only means an author has—an acknowledgment in the preface. I am particularly grateful to Mr. John Knowles, who supplied details in the Chronology about the correct sequence of biographical events. Mr. Paul Sadler, editorial director at Phillips Exeter and a former classmate of Knowles, also provided useful information about the effect of World War II on the Exeter School and its students. The library staff of Phillips Exeter was of great help as well, and I would like to thank Mr. Edouard L. Desrochers, Academy Archivist, for allowing me to examine the manuscript of *A Separate Peace,* which is owned by the school, and for calling my attention to many publications that bear on the school's history between 1942 and 1945, the period when Knowles was a student.

Thanks are due to my typist, Irene Kokkala, whose expertise with the word processor saved me much time and labor. Finally I am indebted as always to my wife, Jon Lee, for her able assistance with proofing and for her encouragement.

John Knowles.
Photograph by Jimm Roberts.

Chronology: John Knowles's Life and Works

1926	Born 16 September in the coal mining town of Fairmont, West Virginia, population 29,000. The third child of James Myron and Mary Beatrice Shea Knowles.
1932–41	Attends public schools through the ninth grade in his hometown.
1942	Enters Phillips Exeter Academy in New Hampshire for the fall term as a tenth grader or "lower middler," as sophomores are called at Exeter. Resides in a house occupied by a house master's family and six boys, rather than in a dormitory. Finds the academic requirements very rigorous and feels that school is intellectually intimidating and socially cold.
1943	Attends a special summer wartime session called the Anticipatory Program. Belongs to a group known as the Suicide Society where members jump from a tree into a river. Injures his foot and is on crutches after a bad fall.
1944–45	Graduates early from preparatory school in August 1944 with an "English" diploma and enters Yale for the 1944 fall term prior to going into U.S. Army Air Force. Assigned to the aviation cadet program; spends eight months in preflight program at bases in Texas and Illinois before his discharge from the service in November 1945.
1946	Reenters Yale University and resides in Pierson College, a residence hall presided over by Professor Gordon S. Haight. Makes the varsity swimming team.
1947	Starts to submit stories to the *Yale Record*, the college humor magazine. Is invited to join Yale's Whiffenpoofs but is not tapped for Skull and Bones, the Yale secret society he hoped to belong to.
1948	Applies to the Yale *Daily*, the undergraduate-produced newspaper, and is accepted as a "heeler," a job requiring proofread-

ing, interviewing, and even delivering papers. Eventually elected to the editorial board and given the prestigious-sounding post of editorial secretary.

1949   Presents a novel to the faculty as his senior essay at Yale. Graduates with a B.A. degree in English.

1950–52   Works as a reporter and drama critic for the *Hartford Courant,* Hartford, Connecticut. The Korean War starts but Knowles is not recalled to military duty.

1952–56   Tours England, Italy, and southern France. Writes first novel, *Descent to Proselito,* which is accepted for publication but withdrawn upon the advice of Thornton Wilder. Returns to the United States and earns living as a free-lance journalist; shares an apartment in New York City's Hell's Kitchen district with actor Bradford Dillman. Contributes several articles to *Holiday* magazine, including a piece on his alma mater, "Yale Man," in the May 1953 issue and a description of his native state, West Virginia, in the October issue of the same year.

1953   Publishes first story, "A Turn in the Sun," in *Story Magazine.*

1956   In May *Cosmopolitan* publishes a short story entitled "Phineas," which contained material that formed the basis for the early chapters of *A Separate Peace.* Makes his first return to Exeter as an alumnus, eleven years after his graduation.

1956–60   Becomes a member of the editorial staff of *Holiday* and moves to Philadelphia. Writes pieces for the "Lively Arts" section and contributes two signed articles: one entitled "A Naturally Superior School" about Phillips Exeter that appears in the December 1956 issue and the other about his experiences on the French Riviera, entitled "Cold Plunge into Skin Divings," in the June 1956 issue. At age twenty-eight he starts work on his third novel, which would become *A Separate Peace.*

1958   Vacations in southern France and takes up the then-novel sport of skin diving while at Cape d'Antibes. Meets and gets advice on the subject from Jacques Cousteau himself.

1959   British edition of *A Separate Peace* is published by Secker and Warbury. Receives favorable notices from London reviewers.

1960   American edition of *A Separate Peace* issued by Macmillan appears 29 February on leap year day, after being turned down by eleven publishers. Sells 7,000 copies in first printing and receives critical acclaim. Wins the Rosenthal Award from the National Institute of Arts and Letters and the William Faulkner Award for the most promising first novel of 1960.

Chronology: John Knowles's Life and Works

1960   *A Separate Peace* is nominated for the National Book Award. The success of the novel allows Knowles to resign his post with *Holiday* and become a full-time fiction writer. Leaves the United States and travels extensively abroad, making visits to Lebanon, Syria, Jordan, and Greece.

1962   Publishes a second novel, *Morning in Antibes,* which drew from his experiences on the Riviera in 1958. The reviews of the book are almost totally negative. Contributes an essay, "The Young Writer's Real Friends," to the *New York Times Book Review.*

1963–64   Invited by the faculty of the University of North Carolina at Chapel Hill to serve as writer-in-residence.

1964   Publishes *Double Vision: American Thoughts Abroad,* a collection of essays reflecting his experiences in the Middle East.

1965   An essay entitled "The Writer in Residence" appears in the *New York Times,* detailing his experiences in that capacity.

1966   His third novel, *Indian Summer,* a Literary Guild Selection, is dedicated to his creative writing mentor, Thornton Wilder.

1968–69   Invited to be writer-in-residence at Princeton University. Publishes a collection of short stories entitled *Phineas: Six Stories.*

1970   Takes up year-round residence in Southampton, New York, near a community of writers that includes Truman Capote, Willy Morris, and Irwin Shaw.

1971   *The Paragon,* his fourth novel, appears, published by Random House.

1972   Motion picture adaptation of *A Separate Peace* is released by Hollywood.

1974   *Spreading Fires,* a novel, is published by Random House.

1978   *A Vein of Riches,* a historical novel based on the coal industry in West Virginia, is published by Little, Brown.

1981   *Peace Breaks Out,* a sequel to *A Separate Peace,* returns to the preparatory school scene with a different cast of characters.

1986   *The Private Life of Axie Reed* is published by E. P. Dutton.

1988   Resides in Fort Lauderdale, Florida, and is currently at work on his autobiography.

CHAPTER 1

Historical Context

A Separate Peace can be read as a war novel; in fact, the title comes from another war novel, Hemingway's *A Farewell to Arms,* a book in which the protagonist, Lt. Frederic Henry, declares his own private armistice during World War I. Knowles does not deal with the actual conflict of the battlefield. Rather, it is the impact of the war on the lives of schoolboys who are not yet involved in the combat that is the subject of *A Separate Peace.* The social upheaval the war caused is noted by the novel's narrator, Gene Forrester:

> Everyone has a moment in history which belongs particularly to him. It is the moment when his emotions achieve their most powerful sway over him, and afterward when you say to this person "the world today" or "life" or "reality" he will assume that you mean this moment, even if it is fifty years past. The world, through his unleashed emotions, imprinted itself upon him, and he carries the stamp of that passing moment forever.
>
> For me, this moment—four years is a moment in history—was the war. The war was and is reality for me. I still instinctively live and think in its atmosphere. These are some of its characteristics: Franklin Delano Roosevelt is the President of the United States, and he always has been. The other two eternal world leaders are Win-

1

ston Churchill and Josef Stalin. America is not, never has been, and never will be what the songs and poems call it, a land of plenty. Nylon, meat, gasoline, and steel are rare. There are too many jobs and not enough workers. Money is very easy to earn but rather hard to spend, because there isn't very much to buy. Trains are always late and always crowded with "servicemen." The war will always be fought very far from America and it will never end. . . . The prevailing color of life in America is a dull, dark green called olive drab. That color is always respectable and always important. Most other colors risk being unpatriotic.

It is this special America, a very untypical one I guess, an unfamiliar transitional blur in the memories of most people, which is the real America for me.[1]

The war that Gene means is, of course, World War II, a war fought nearly half a century ago. Although it is an epoch still within the living memory of millions of Americans, the nation has since fought two limited, undeclared, and unpopular wars in Korea and Vietnam, and it is difficult for many people to understand that World War II was different. Perhaps the incongruous phrase that Studs Terkel took for the title of his oral history of World War II distinguishes this war from all other wars in that it was—and is yet—thought of as the "good war."[2]

Even though young people in this country never experienced World War II as a hardship the way European and Asian children did, the young of America grew up in a special atmosphere that, though far removed from the battlefields, always reminded them that a war was on. Of all age groups in the United States, it was the boys who were not quite draft age who were the most preoccupied by the war. There was no thought, as in the case of Korea or Vietnam, of avoiding military service; the big question was when they would go and in which branch they would serve. Gene Forrester points out that there was a special significance attached to being sixteen years old. "Sixteen is the key and crucial and natural age for the human being. . . . When you are sixteen, adults are slightly impressed and almost intimidated by you. This is a puzzle, finally solved by the realization that they foresee your military future, fighting for them" (33). Thus, the war changed the way the older and younger generations felt about each other. For instance, at Devon the faculty grew more tolerant of the boys' behavior because, as Gene says, "I think we reminded them of what peace was like, we boys of sixteen. We were registered with no draft board, we had taken no physical examinations. . . . We were careless and wild, and I suppose we could be thought of as a sign of the life the war was being fought to preserve. Anyway, they were more indulgent toward us than at any other time. . . . They noticed our games tolerantly. We reminded them of what peace was like, of lives which were not bound up with destruction" (17).

In addition to the attitude of tolerance toward youth, the quality of life in America's exclusive preparatory schools suddenly changed in numerous and often significant ways. Knowles, commenting on the conditions at Phillips Exeter during the war in a 1972 interview with the editors of the *Exonian,* the Phillips Exeter school newspaper, remarked that, following Pearl Harbor, nearly all the school's younger faculty were away in service or doing war-related jobs. He added that, except for a few younger men who were 4-F, or unfit for military service, all of the teachers were between fifty and seventy years old. Thus, there were no younger teachers for the boys to take as role models, and the students had only one another to turn to for close friendships. The faculty, in addition to being older than was usual, were in many cases not even regular Exeter staff but substitutes brought in from other schools or from retirement for the duration. These men did not fully grasp the historical or social traditions of the school, and this also distanced them from the boys.[3]

In another item from the school paper, Professor Howard T. Easton, a teacher at Exeter during the 1940s, recollected that another effect of the war on the school was an increase in class size, which threatened a sacred tradition at Phillips Exeter—the "Harkness Plan," an arrangement that limits the class size to a dozen or so students who meet the teacher in a seminar situation around a table. Students also had to work harder, Professor Easton said, because the academic program was accelerated through a plan called the Anticipatory Program, which graduated boys before they reached the draft age of eighteen, thereby allowing them at least to complete their secondary school education before entering the service.[4] This special program was set up in several of the nation's top prep schools, following directives from the War Department in 1942; its intention was to keep boys in school and, at the same time, provide the teaching and training recommended by the armed services. Thus, students at Phillips Exeter who were accepted into the Anticipatory Program had to study more trigonometry, physics, American history, and modern foreign languages than prescribed by the normal curriculum. Also, first aid training, Morse code, and rifle marksmanship were added as classes. Although there is no mention that military-style obstacle courses were set up, the school's emphasis on athletics and interest in sports probably answered the requirements of a sound mind and a healthy body.[5]

The plan of the Anticipatory Program was to do the equivalent academic work of the senior year with a special summer session of ten weeks' duration that ran from late June until September. Although the program was not mandatory, it was recommended to all boys who qualified. The first accelerated class at Exeter began in the summer of 1943 and was open to boys who would reach their eighteenth birthdays by February 1944; it enrolled sixty-four students. Those in the Anticipatory Program received diplomas in August or February as well as June, depending on how they cycled through.

In addition to changing the academic calendar, the war imposed numerous smaller adaptations. For example, there were meatless meals in the dining halls and no candy at the canteen. Worst of all, Exeter boys lost their maid service and had to housekeep their own rooms, as the defense industry drew off the supply of available female help. The authorities were apprehensive that the curtailing of this service might cause an adverse reaction among the boys, but they were delighted that its loss was instead taken in the spirit of the times, although the boys had to get up earlier in the mornings to accomplish their domestic chores before breakfast.

The students at Phillips Exeter Academy, like Americans everywhere, were contributing to the war effort by raising money for war bonds or volunteering their services. With money raised by the boys, an ambulance was purchased for the Red Cross. They also donated blood weekly to the local hospital, manned aircraft observation posts (two of which were maintained on towers at either end of the town of Exeter), and engaged in labor duties in the community, helping harvest the apple crop and shovel snow off the railroad tracks to keep the line open for trains carrying troops and war materials. For these community services they received five dollars a day and a free box lunch and were given credit for physical education.[6]

Other signs of the war were blackout curtains on dormitory windows and frequent air raid drills during the early months of 1942. Gasoline rationing and tire shortages meant fewer visits from parents and less travel to and from school in automobiles. Apparently, no detachment of troops was ever actually billeted on the campus, and the occupation of the school that Knowles describes near the end of *A Separate Peace* is purely imaginary. Paul Sadler, the editorial director of the Communications Office at Phillips Exeter Academy and a classmate of Knowles during the war years, reports that most of *A Separate Peace* is very true to the historical record except for the detail about the parachute riggers school. The war did finally make itself felt upon the lives of many of the young men in ways that were more serious than the temporary inconveniences of food shortages, accelerated schedules, crowded classes, and work for the war effort. Between 1942 and 1945 the war was an inevitability for all those of draft age; some 3,200 Exeter men answered the call to arms, and out of that number 154 lost their lives. The alumni magazines of the Exeter school during the World War II years carry pictures and poignant accounts of the deaths of many of those young men, whose futures were full of promise but were cut short by war, which, as Knowles so powerfully reveals in *A Separate Peace*, is the result of something ignorant in the human heart.

So the one thing that most young men in America could count on was that by the time they were eighteen their lives would be disrupted by military service. Unless they were seriously handicapped physically or mentally, they would be classified by their draft board as 1-A, fit for military service. The need for manpower was so great that by 1943 all the services—army, air force, navy, and even the marines—were calling up draftees. Most, however, would go into the army and usually be assigned to the infantry. It was a time, as Knowles writes, when "the prevailing color of life in America is a dull, dark green called olive drab. That color is always respectable and always important" (33). The army was so desperate that it even took illiterates and had nearly half a million men in uniform who could not write their names or read at all. Anyone who could understand enough English to be sworn in was considered fit for service. Only those men who stood under five feet tall and weighed less than 105 pounds, or lacked more than half their teeth, or were more than fifty percent blind would be classified 4-F, or unfit for duty. Surprisingly, the major cause for rejection by the army was not physical handicaps or illiteracy but emotional distur-bance. Some three million American men would be excused from ser-vice because of mental instability. The reasons for the large numbers suffering from anxiety have never been adequately explained, but the author Phillip Wylie blamed the situation on "momism," his term for excessive coddling of sons by overprotective mothers. This premise was given credence by a psychiatric study undertaken by Dr. Edward Strecker for the Secretary of War; in his findings Dr. Strecker observed that many mothers had not weaned their offspring emotionally.[7]

The character Erwin Lepellier in *A Separate Peace* seems to be an example of this type of youth; unable to adjust to the realities of army life, he deserts after undergoing a nervous breakdown. Ironically, "Leper," as he is nicknamed, had not balked at going into the service; in fact, he enlisted, imagining that military life would be as clean and pure as the recruiting films about the ski troops that he had seen. As a result of Leper's experience, Gene and his classmate Brinker Hadley are not as naive and make plans to enter branches of the service, such as the navy and the coast guard, that will not be as dirty and danger-ous as the army (191).

Whatever service a young man wound up in, the arrival at the "reception centers," as the recruit camps were called, was a shock. Most were crude, temporary outposts that had been put up on land that had no civilian purpose. Thus, drill fields and barracks were set down in the swamps of Louisiana, on the deserts of Texas, and in the frozen drill fields of the Great Lakes. If the climate was not hostile enough, there was the alien atmosphere of military life to further disorient the new servicemen. Their heads were shaved, they were issued ill-fitting uniforms, and they found themselves stabbed with hypodermic needles while being shouted at and cursed by gruff, non-commissioned officers. They were far from the insulation of family, friends, and home; it is no wonder that many developed psychological problems.

The loss of civilian identity was a traumatic experience for many, and it was particularly difficult for the better-educated trainees. College men, especially, had the most trouble adjusting to military life. Some would escape the brutality of the barracks by going to officer training school or being selected to attend the navy's V-12 or the army's ASTP schools located on college campuses, but most would not be so lucky since, as the war wore on, the army needed more riflemen than officers.[8] Men who were accustomed to finer things had to get used to hillbilly music, profanity, and the lack of anything resembling culture. Most post libraries stocked only westerns, thrillers, or sexy romances; the scarcity of decent reading matter seemed at times like official policy—deeper reading might make soldiers think.

Furthermore, the sergeants, petty officers, and company level officers who supervised the basic and boot camps did not always represent the highest traditions of the service; often they were men returned from the battlefronts for incompetence or injuries. At times, the treatment they dealt out to recruits was criminal, even by military standards.

Going off to war, then, was not the romantic experience recruits expected, and the military's attempts to transform civilians into soldiers in eight weeks of training were not always heroic. In *A Separate Peace* Knowles creates a double vision of the war years. We see events as Gene saw them from 1942 to 1943, when the war did not seem to be such a bad thing, creating a more permissive atmosphere at the academy, providing them with new forms of recreation such as leaping from the tree and playing blitzball (a game invented by Finny) and allowing them to miss classes to shovel snow off the railroads or to help farmers harvest crops. But by the time of Gene's graduation in 1943, his attitude toward the war changes. He realizes that wars are the result of defects in our human nature rather than grand crusades, and he hopes to defer going into combat by staying in training schools as long as possible. The novel ends with Gene going off to the navy, but, as he tells us, he missed all the killing.

Though he escapes the actual warfare, Gene's war memories are with him forever. As he says, this moment in history put its stamp on him permanently. For him this was the time of the real America.

Chapter 2

The Importance of the Work

John Knowles's *A Separate Peace* has enjoyed the status of a minor classic for over a quarter of a century. It is a book that has acquired, as Knowles himself noted, a "destiny apart" from his own. He has continued to write novels and to date has published nine works of fiction, but nothing has equalled the prizes and the praise that have been accorded *A Separate Peace*. Long after the warm reception of the reviewers and the analyses of the critics, the continuing appeal of the book is registered by ongoing high sales. It has become a literary legacy, passed down from one generation of readers to the next, and it is mostly young people who read and treasure *A Separate Peace*. Some come to it because it is required reading for school, others because it has been recommended by a friend, teacher, or parent. In an *Esquire* article published on the twenty-fifth anniversary of the novel, Knowles said that *A Separate Peace* had become a "public property" about which people talked "proprietarily;" they looked askance "if I murmur a dissent as to their view of my work and they go on to explain what it is really about."[9]

The story told in *A Separate Peace* is not the usual stuff of bestsellers, and, aside from the fact that the protagonists are all young boys, it is not obvious at first why it would appeal to young people. The purpose of the book, Knowles confided, was to unscramble, plumb, and explain what had happened during a very "peculiar summer" at Phillips Exeter Academy in New Hampshire when he was a sixteen-year-old summer session student in 1943. What began as a story of two schoolboys became an allegory about the causes of war. Through his words in A Separate Peace, Knowles revealed emotions and thoughts that he himself experienced, especially how he and his generation, who were facing the prospect of a world war, felt about participating in violence and aggression. Moreover, Knowles has said he tried to answer questions concerning loyalty and rivalry, goodness and hate, fear and idealism—all of which were issues "swirling around us that peculiar summer." The book was written "to dramatize and work through those questions."

While there is much that is unique or peculiar about the situation described in the novel—it takes place at an exclusive private school during an unusual moment of history and concerns characters who come from privileged families—there is, nevertheless, an appeal about A Separate Peace that transcends all these externals. The emotional truth that the novel communicates to readers is that we all lose something in the process of growing up. Knowles's moral message is as simple and as complex as William Blake's in the Songs of Innocence and Experience. The two sixteen-year-olds, Gene and Finny, who are the central characters, represent respectively what Blake called "the contrary states" of human nature. Gene, the incipient intellectual, has the habit of always analyzing his and the other people's motives; he is also selfish, egocentric, and prideful. Finny, on the other hand, is nonintellectual, altruistic, and without a trace of vanity. In their basic character traits, the two match almost point for point Blake's paradigm of the unfallen and fallen states of mankind, which he called experience and innocence. Gene's absorption in his own "selfhood" is foiled off against the "selfless" Finny. The first defines himself by books and high marks in school; the other knows himself through sports and actions. Gene's life is governed by prudence and premeditation, Finny's by spontaneity and emotion.

Gene's transgression against Finny is the central event of the novel. Everything that follows is, as Knowles has said, "one long abject confession, a *mea culpa*, a tale of crime—if a crime has been committed—and of no punishment. It is a story of growth through tragedy."[10] The implication of Knowles's remarks is that the response to his book is conditioned by the fact that so many young people feel guilty about something in their experience, be it a betrayal of a friend or simply shame for growing up. Thus, because *A Separate Peace* touches on an experience common to so many and because it suggests that the sin or shame may be overcome, it has influenced the lives of millions of readers.

Finally, when assessing a literary work's reputation as a masterwork, it should be pointed out that books do not achieve such status because of favorable comments or approving critiques, or even because of huge annual sales figures. While a consensus among critics and reviewers about the "greatness" of literary productions will go a long way toward establishing the reputation of an author or a title, Knowles's novel transcends all these considerations. As we have seen, *A Separate Peace* makes a strong emotional and intellectual impression for the reasons that Knowles himself has so succinctly stated above. But some of the impact of the novel is due certainly to the rich reading experience it provides. Knowles's carefully crafted prose is both simple and profound. Almost every page reveals a command of the resources of the language; an evocative, almost poetic prose, the use of images and symbols, and a controlled tone of nostalgia are the hallmarks of Knowles's literary style. Although *A Separate Peace* is a beautifully written book whose style and imagery rank it with the very best of American novels since World War II, it is, finally, a profoundly disturbing work, whose interpretation is incremented by time and experience, yielding meanings long after the immediate impact of reading is behind us.

CHAPTER 3

Critical Reception

For a book that has sold over nine million copies to date, Knowles's first novel did not have an auspicious start. In the *Esquire* article mentioned earlier, Knowles described the way the novel was written and his subsequent attitude toward the book that is now a classic and has become frequently required schoolroom reading, making it a title that many people have heard about and—in this case—actually read.

The novel was begun in 1954 when Knowles was twenty-eight years old and living in Philadelphia, Pennsylvania, where he worked as an editor for *Holiday* magazine. The writing of the manuscript came quickly for him, he says, flowing from his mind and into words with great ease. He worked on a regular schedule while composing the novel: going to bed at midnight, rising at seven, washing his face, having orange juice and coffee for breakfast, writing for an hour and turning out five to six hundred words, and then going to work. "No book can have been easier to get down on paper," he admits, adding, " . . . *A Separate Peace* wrote itself."[11]

Knowles turned the book over to a literary agent, who circulated the manuscript among some of the most prestigious publishers in the United States. After being read by some of the best editors in the business, it was rejected by eleven publishers. All the readers who saw the book apparently felt as Knowles himself did: "Who's going to want to read about a bunch of prep schoolboys and what happened to them long ago in the past?" Knowles, however, did think that the book was good enough to be published, although he did not believe it would interest more than a few thousand readers at best.

In 1959 the rights to *A Separate Peace* were picked up by the London publishing firm Secker and Warburg, who brought out the British edition. The book's reception by the literary press in England was enthusiastic; almost every review was positive. The most important notice was published in the *Times* of London, appearing in the pages of the "Literary Supplement" section for 1 May 1959. It called *A Separate Peace* "a novel of altogether exceptional power and distinction." The reviewer, focusing on the characterizations of Gene and Finny, praised Knowles for creating a "vital contrast" in his description of their relationship and admired the precision and economy with which the setting was handled.

Other favorable reviews soon followed in the major papers and journals, such as *Manchester Guardian, New Statesman* and *Spectator*. The reviewer for the *Guardian*, Ann Duchene, liked the way Knowles drew with "tenderness and restraint" the affection between the two boys and his representation of their "laconic, fantastic" schoolboy idiom. Maurice Richardson, writing a less favorable notice for the *New Statesman*, applauded Knowles for his "pleasing variations from conventional American attitudes," especially the pretense that wars do not exist. He found what he called "NeoForsterian and Trillingnesque" lines of modeling in the novel, but concluded that the writing, though pleasing, did not quite convince because the school background was not as fully drawn as he felt "institutional frameworks" should be. One of the most interesting British reviews was written for the *Spectator* by Simon Raven, who, while labeling *A Separate Peace* a modest book, emphasized the novel's wider theme, which he took to be pacifism. *A Separate Peace* was called a timely book by another reviewer, because of the greater need in 1959 than in 1942 for its sort of practical, commonsense protest against war. The real power of

Knowles's novel, this English reviewer said, was the example it provided of "individuals disassociating themselves from the follies of others." E. M. Forster and Angus Wilson also added their praise of the book to the chorus of approval from the British literary establishment. Looking back now at the way *A Separate Peace* was regarded in England in the spring of 1959, it is possible to discern two reactions by the critics. The reviewers in the left-wing press responded to the novel's antiwar sentiments, which were appreciated in an American author, especially during these years when the Dulles doctrine of massive nuclear response was creating cold war anxiety. On the other hand, conservative reviewers approved of the novel's treatment of original sin and redemption and saw Knowles's book as a contender for the best American novel since J. D. Salinger's *Catcher in the Rye.* All concurred in their praise of the novel, albeit for different reasons.

Following the favorable reception of *A Separate Peace* in England, several publishers in the United States showed interest in the book. Macmillan bought the rights and brought out the American edition on 29 February 1960. The first review was by Edmund Fuller in a prepublication notice for the *New York Times* that appeared in the Sunday literary supplement on 9 February. Fuller was unequivocal in his admiration, calling Knowles a writer "already skilled in craft and discerning in his perceptions." Recognizing that Devon was modelled after Exeter Academy, he disallowed the importance of the institutional setting, saying that the school situation was not integral to or a prominent part of the novel. The World War II background was identified as more central to the action because of the anxieties it created and the decisions that the boys would be required to make on account of it; it was the events beyond the campus that "loom large in the psychological structure of the novel." The only caveat Fuller made concerned the plot, which contained several episodes that were not totally convincing to him; nevertheless, the book's "major truths" overrode his objections to the structure. Numerous reviews appeared in March 1960, following the book's publication. One of the more important ones was written by Granville Hicks in *Saturday Review* and entitled "The Good Have a Quiet Heroism." Hicks commended Knowles for his portayal of a virtuous character, noting that Finny, the sixteen-year-old prep schoolboy, was not an apparent choice for a hero. He disagreed with English critics who compared Finny with Holden Caulfield, J. D. Salinger's protagonist of *Catcher in the Rye,* and argued that Finny's impulsiveness and unconventionality were not, like Holden's, a form of protest against authority or a mode of self-assertion, but was rather a facet of his personality. His review concluded with the view that "the more one thinks about the character, the more meaning he has" and opined that, were it not for Finny, we would soon forget *A Separate Peace* as a diverting but affecting tale about boyhood tragedy. Instead, "he sticks in our minds," Hicks said.

Most of the early reviews were carried in newspapers, and those in the major city papers were largely favorable. The *New York Tribune* called *A Separate Peace* a "consistently admirable exercise in the craft of fiction—disciplined, precise, witty and completely conscious of intention,"—the intention being the revelation of the psychological pressures of war on boys too young to understand it. The book reviewer for *Chicago Sunday Tribune* noted that the perspective of a fifteen-year narrative provided a way to make the most of a plot that had only one dramatic incident, but faulted the ending of the novel for its inclusiveness. Douglas Aitken's review in the *San Fransisco Chronicle* was full of praise for Knowles; he had no reservations whatever and ranked the novel with the work of the best young American novelists of the day, such as William Styron. He praised the book for its prose style and imagery while eschewing "the false symbolism which so many writers employ in an attempt to add depth to their work." Aitken went on to say, "Knowles has written a book that has great depth of meaning which should be read by every person who likes to think about a book after reading it."

During the late spring and summer months of 1960, positive reviews continued to appear in literary journals and national news magazines. Whitney Balliet, in a perceptive article for *New Yorker,* called attention to the scriptural allegory and Greek mythology employed in *A Separate Peace.* He credited Knowles for not writing in the manner of J. D. Salinger and concluded with the view that it was an "estimable book, which deserves the distinction it has achieved." In an unsigned review in *Time,* entitled "The Lead," more appreciation was registered for *A Separate Peace.* The *Time* book critic found a parallel between Knowles's detachment from his hero-narrator and Stephen Crane's unsentimental handling of his protagonist in *The Red Badge of Courage.* Furthermore, the two novels were similar not only in kind but also in quality. Having said so much to the credit of Knowles, the review concluded that the implications of the novel were too varied and too subtle to insist on single explication; the book was, however, certainly saying that the thing we all destroy finally is our own innocence. William F. Buckley, surprisingly, also liked *A Separate Peace,* given the liberal cast of the book's theme on war. In his review, Buckley praised Knowles for avoiding the "psychoanalytical cant and sexual grime" of Salinger's *Catcher in the Rye.* He hoped that *A Separate Peace* was indicative of a sign of reviving health in the "preponderant literature of youth" that had to date risen from "a fever swamp." The notice in *Harper's* was prophetic, with the reviewer predicting that the book would win a large audience. Alfred Kazin's review in *Reporter* focused on the novel's two central characters, who he says were created with such completeness that they "break from the author's discretion and shaping, attaining a felt and almost unreachable life of their own." In one of the few negative appraisals, Marvin Mudrick in *Hudson Review* accused Knowles of "self-indulgent toying with thought and language for the purpose of suggesting big issues and unplumbable wisdom." He was also disappointed in the way Finny's character was drawn, saying his nature was only asserted and that Knowles's efforts to make him come alive were inept. Unlike many other readers, Mudrick liked the nightmarish trial episode, which he called the only achieved scene in *A Separate Peace.* Likewise, the *Commonweal* reviewer spoke of *A Separate Peace* in slighting terms, writing the novel off as "one more foray into the territory of guilt earned in adolescence" that did not deserve the comparisons made with Salinger's *Catcher in the Rye.*

Thus, although the reviews of the book upon its publication were generally favorable, it never became a best-seller, nor was it selected by any book clubs. It did, however, sell seven thousand copies in the first printing, and the paperback rights were acquired by Dell Publishers; it eventually passed into paperback as a Bantam book. The most notable tribute that came to Knowles was when *A Separate Peace* was named the recipient of the William Faulkner Foundation Award.

Knowles was pleased with the excellent notices and with the sales, which he had not expected to be more than three thousand copies. But "that seemed to be that . . . and then it was as though a wave, a very large wave, was gathering force, and moving toward me. There was a far-off rumbling coming nearer; letters, then more letters began to arrive from readers, then teachers took the book up by the thousands, and the sales climbed and climbed."[12]

The first academic assessments of *A Separate Peace* were made by a younger generation of English teachers, who were excited by the discovery of the novel and wanted to show its possibilities for classroom use. Articles started to appear that discussed the issues involved with teaching *A Separate Peace,* such as theme, structure, and symbolism. Some teachers who had been inhibited about requiring students to read Salinger's *Catcher in the Rye* because of objections from parents and the community to its use of obscene words saw that *A Separate Peace* provided a viable alternative to the proscriptions imposed on *Catcher in the Rye.* John K. Crabbe, in an article entitled "In the Playing Fields of Devon," published in 1963, recommended the novel to high school teachers of American literature for classroom use. He advocated including the novel in the syllabus because he saw it as both an instructive and an entertaining work of fiction. The treatment of the theme of American innocence, he said, was akin to Hemingway's in the Nick Adams stories and to Fitzgerald's in *The Great Gatsby,* providing possibilities for initiating classroom discussion. Crabbe also pointed out how the major and minor characters represented types of people whose problems students could relate to. Finally, the book's brevity, simple language, and interesting plot made it ideal classroom material from both the students' and the teachers' points of view.

Another important early essay that helped to establish the reputation of *A Separate Peace* was written by James Ellis in 1964. Ellis analyzed the innocence theme and the interconnection of the book's symbols—two seasons, two rivers, and war and peace.

Throughout the 1960s there was a constant stream of articles on *A Separate Peace,* with one or two every year or so appearing in the critical quarterlies and scholarly journals, and with each devoted to some facet of interpretation, analysis, or evaluation. But, like the reviews, which played out after a year following publication, the critical commentary all but ceased after the decade ended, and the academic community seemed satisfied that the meaning and merits of the novel had been adequately explicated and assimilated. After all, how much interpretation does a 183-page work of fiction require? Although the critical responses to the book have not been continuous, they have from the first been admiring and appreciative, and *A Separate Peace* has stood up well under the scrutiny. The criticism has abated, but the novel continues to attract readers and has now gone through seventy printings, with 7,445,000 copies of the Bantam edition in print. Average sales through the years have been between 250,000 and 400,000 per year, bringing Knowles anywhere from $30,000 to $40,000 in royalties each year for a quarter of a century. So, the first book that John Knowles ever wrote has not only won him critical praise, literary prizes, and the admiration of millions of readers; it has provided him with an annuity for life.

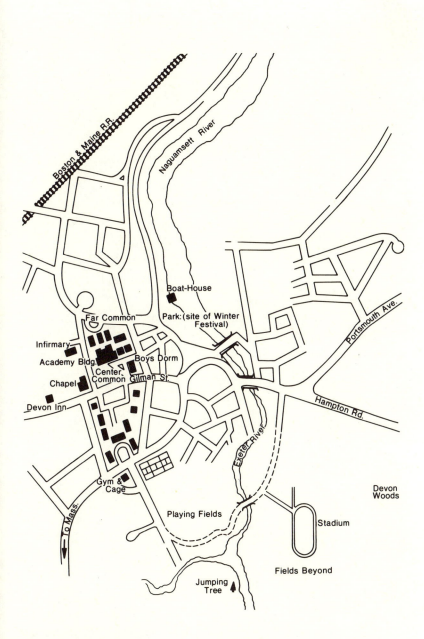

Map of Devon School.
Reconstructed with the assistance of John Knowles and Phillips Exeter Academy.

a reading

CHAPTER 4

The Scene

Several things are obvious from a study of the chapter outlines and the original manuscript of *A Separate Peace:* the author had an early grasp of the nature and motivations of his characters, he had decided on the general sequence of events, and his own attitude toward the material was already shaped. For one thing, by the time he started to compose the novel, Knowles had to some degree formed a notion of the history of his main characters. In May 1956, Knowles published a short story entitled "Phineas," which, in a much more compressed form, covers the events of the novel's opening chapters from the first jump up to Finny's injury.[13] It deals with events of the summer at Devon but does not go beyond the episode at the tree. The story does, however, use the same flashback-framing device. It opens with Gene standing in front of the door to Finny's bedroom in his hometown, where Gene has come to visit his convalescing friend. The scene shifts back in time by three months to the beginning of the summer, when Finny and Gene become roommates and good friends at Devon School.

As in the novel, one of Finny's prominent characteristics is his unusual baritone voice. Finny's attitude is outgoing and forthright; he divulges his beliefs about God, religion, and girls at their first meeting, while the more diffident Gene reserves comment on such confidential matters. The upshot of Finny's disarming candor is to make Gene feel inadequate and dull-witted, "as though he had never had an original thought. . . ." The sectional differences in the two boys are also stressed in the short story. Gene's southern accent and his lime-green, short-sleeved sports shirt with the bottom squared and worn outside the pants, although much admired in the South, are not the eastern prep school fashion. Like the novel, Gene's suspicious nature is established by his resentment of Finny's attempt to "yank out all my thoughts and feelings and scatter them around underfoot" as he has scattered the clothes from his suitcase. Finny is described as a person with many foibles: his inability to sing on-key, his amazing way of dressing, and his poor showing as a student. Another detail in the story that reappears later in the novel is Finny's pink shirt, which he wears to class to "memorialize" the bombing of Ploesti oil fields. He wears it on several other occasions in the story to italicize other victories—a grade of C on a history test, the retirement of the school dietitian, and the battle of Midway. The shirt is thus already used by Knowles as more than an item of apparel; it is an emblem of Finny's special psychological makeup. As in the novel, Gene dons this shirt in the aftermath of the accident when he dresses in Finny's clothing.

Finny is an excellent athlete, but he has the odd notion that an athlete is "naturally good at everything at once." He participates in games like soccer, hockey, and lacrosse, disdaining those more prestigious sports like football where the plays are preordained and have a geometrical order. His personal athletic code demands a sport where the players are free to create, to invent without any previous plan. An enmity develops between Gene and his roommate because Gene supposes that Finny, who is the best athlete and most popular boy in school, is interfering with Gene's studies to drag him down to Finny's academic level. The last part of the short story deals with the boys jumping from the tree, the formation of the super suicide society, and Gene's treachery.

Incidentally, Knowles has confirmed in a *New York Times* interview that there was a Super Suicide Society while he was at Exeter whose members made jumps into the river.[14] Although no one was ever seriously injured while making leaps such as those described in the story, Knowles himself got a cut as a result of a jump and was on crutches most of the summer of 1943.

In almost every respect the short story is an abstract of the first six chapters of the novel. One evening Finny, the narrator, and three other boys go to the river with the intention of jumping from a tree that leans out over the river's edge. Finny jumps into the river impetuously, expecting the others to follow. Everybody refuses except the narrator, who "hated" the idea but jumps anyway because he does not want to be outdone by Phineas. Phineas has the idea to form the "Super Suicide Society of the Summer Session," inscribing his name and the narrator's as chapter members, and enrolling Chet, Bobby, and Leper as trainees. The society meets almost every evening, and all members are required to attend and jump.

Before a French examination, Phineas goes to the narrator's room and asks him to attend a meeting of the Suicide Society because Leper has finally agreed to jump. Gene, although irritated, agrees to go, saying sarcastically, "Okay, we go. We watch little lily-liver Leper not jump from a tree, and I ruin my grade." Finny is taken aback at this and says simply, "I didn't know you needed to study. . . . I thought it just came to you." The narrator realizes for the first time that Phineas had assumed that the narrator's intellectual capacity came as easily as his own natural ability at sports. Truth dawns on the narrator, and he understands that Phineas has never been jealous of him or considered him a rival. This realization that Finny is so superior to him causes the narrator to shake the tree's limb, making Phineas fall into the river with a "sickening natural thud." One of his legs is shattered in the fall and Phineas is maimed for life.

Afterwards, when the narrator goes to see Phineas at the infirmary, his guilt almost makes him reveal the truth. When he asks Phineas if he remembers how he fell, Phineas answers, "I just fell, that's all." The narrator finally realizes that he has not been jealous of Phineas's popularity, background, or skill at sports—he has envied

Finny's total and complete honesty. The story ends with Gene going to Finny's home in Boston to make a full confession of his guilt.

Knowles make his earliest use of Devon School as the setting for his fiction in a story entitled "A Turn in the Sun."[15] The main character in this story is a boy named Lawrence Stuart, whose anxious nature seems to anticipate that of Gene Forrester. He has the same sense of social insecurity and intense ambition to win academic and athletic distinctions. In both stories there are certain parallels between the fictional events and the experiences of Knowles himself. For instance, Knowles has written that he found Phillips Exeter to be a cold and unfriendly place when he first arrived. He recounts how he arrived there on his birthday, 16 September 1942, and rather than receiving a kind word, was invited in by the house master to listen to a recitation of the school rules.[16] Knowles, like his character, was also displaced by being demoted to the "lower middler" (tenth grade) class rather than entering with his age group as a junior because he was not deemed academically ready to do work at that level at Exeter.

The plot of "A Turn in the Sun" concerns the attempts of Lawrence Stewart to break the barrier of the "foggy social bottomland where unacceptable first year boys dwell." Lawrence, the protagonist, has entered Devon in the fall in the fourth form and instantly finds out that he is not outstanding enough to be accepted by his "sophisticated" peers. He is from an unknown, small Virginia town, he lacks outstanding athletic ability, his clothes are wrong, his vocabulary is common, and he talks about the wrong topics. He is assigned to live in a small house with "six other nebulous flotsam" rather than in a dormitory.

Lawrence, however, soon shows signs of becoming a person to be considered. One day when standing on a bridge, he makes a sudden, unplanned dive into the river, and his dive is so remarkable that when he breaks the surface of the water he has become to his peers a boy to be regarded. His achievement results in an invitation to dinner from Ging Powers, a senior from his own town who, before his dive, had religiously avoided him.

The dinner that evening is Lawrence's downfall. Ironically, he is sure that this is the beginning of a new career at Devon. He meets his host and his friends at a corner table in the Devon Inn. There he is introduced to Vinnie Ump, the vice-chairman of the senior council, and Charles Morrell, an outstanding football, baseball, and hockey player. During the course of the conversation, Lawrence realizes that Ging is a social climber and immediately feels superior to him. He also understands by looking at Morrell that the important aspect of the athlete is not his ability but his unique personality, the "unconscious authority" that his diverse skills give him. Lawrence's visions of being accepted by these campus bigwigs get the better of him and he lies, "I have some cousins, two cousins, you know—they're in clubs at Harvard. . . . " Aware that the others are impressed, Lawrence goes on with his diatribe on the social clubs of Harvard and winds up boasting of his dive from the bridge. When Morrell remarks, "I saw you do it," Lawrence is flattered because the most important athlete in school saw him in his moment of triumph, and he talks excitedly about anything he can think of to make himself sound important. His downfall occurs when he asks which of the men at chapel on the first day of school was the dean; when the other boys describe him, Lawrence responds in his loudest voice, "Like my beagle, that's the way he looks, like the beagle I've got at home, my beagle looks just like that right after he's had a bath." The three seniors then call Lawrence's attention to the elderly couple making their way toward the door; his questions—"Was that the dean? . . . Did he hear me?"—go unanswered, and Lawrence, deeply embarrassed, slips under the table. Only then does Lawrence realize the ridiculousness of his position, "under a table in the Anthony Wayne Dining Room of the Devon Inn, making a fool of himself." Immediately, Ging Morrell and Vinnie make excuses and leave the humiliated Lawrence, his chance to be "regarded" now totally destroyed.

When Lawrence returns to Devon after the spring break, the bleakness of winter has given way to the beauty of early spring. He unaccountably begins to slip in his studies, but in sports he achieves a "minor triumph" when he scores his first goal for his intramural team; the accomplishment, however, does nothing to further his quest to be "regarded." The day of his minor triumph turns out to be the final day of his life. After a shower Lawrence goes to the trophy room and fantasizes that 1954 will be the year that he will win the Fullerton Cup, the trophy awarded to the outstanding athlete of the year. All at once he realizes the "finiteness of the cup" and that with the passage of time the cup and the inscriptions on it will all fade from human memory. The room suddenly feels like a crypt, and he steps outside to the freshness and aroma of spring. That night Lawrence dives from the bridge and drowns in the river. Two classmates who have gone swimming with him try to save him but fail. At a conference two days later one of the boys tells the headmaster that Lawrence "had looked different" before he dived, suggesting the possibility of suicide.

"A Turn in the Sun," like "Phineas," anticipates *A Separate Peace* in style and substance. Structurally, all three plots begin in *medias res;* each work employs a serene setting against which violent or tragic events take place, and each creates a nostalgic atmosphere that is kept up throughout. In "A Turn in the Sun," as in *A Separate Peace,* everything that the characters do is set against the backdrop of changing seasons and the beauties of nature, which—in the naturalistic convention of Hardy and Crane—is indifferent to the human plight. There is also the same use of recurring motifs and important images—the water, the broken heart, the leap, and the quest for acceptance—which figure in both stories as symbols. And, again as in *A Separate Peace,* Devon is made into a microcosmic setting. The use of repetitive scenes figures in the short story as well as in the novel. The two dives from the bridge in "A Turn in the Sun" parallel each other most obviously, the one leading to Lawrence's being "regarded" and the other to his death, and they anticipate the two falls that figure as structural and symbolic devices in *A Separate Peace.*

Another piece of writing that probably informed and shaped Knowles's depiction of life in a New England prep school was the article he wrote for *Holiday* magazine in 1956, which brought him back to the Exeter campus. It doubtlessly caused him to rethink his experiences as a schoolboy and to consider anew the special pressures of spending one's adolescence in a place where the academic, social, and athletic competition complicated an already difficult phase of life.

There are several interesting notations in this article that would strike any reader of *A Separate Peace*. For example, Knowles reveals that Phillips Exeter Academy, unlike the fictional Devon school of the novel, does not have an old school tie, but, aside from this, the parallels between the two schools are readily apparent. He mentions the bell in the high cupola of the Academy Building whose ring could never be forgotten by anyone who has lived there. "It does not joyously peal nor portentously toll. . . . Throughout the school years of Exeter boys the bell rings the changes in their lives." There are other passages in the article that seem to anticipate lines in the novel. Knowles, the returned old grad who is visiting the alma mater for the first time in over a decade, writes: "Then I knew that Exeter hadn't changed. The look of it hadn't changed, I had noticed that at once. In the eleven years since I had graduated there were just a few structures—a long, low maintenance building, an artificial hockey rink, a new art gallery. Nothing to disturb the reminiscing alumnus except a picture-windowed, ranch type someone had tacked onto the simple, venerable first Academy Building. Aside from the outrage it was all as it had been."[17] The same attitude toward the modern modifications in architecture is reflected by the narrator of *A Separate Peace* in his first impressions of the changes that have occurred on the grounds of the Devon school during his absence.

Writing in *Holiday* about the subjective sense of place with which the school endows its students, Knowles says Exeter has a secluded, even provincial quality about it: ". . . I always felt that we were up at the north country, and that our woods extended on into the not-yet-completely-tamed wilderness."[18]

Striking another motif that runs through *A Separate Peace*—that of change in seasons and individuals—Knowles closes out his article with these evocative sentences: "The changes of season are more emphatic than almost anywhere in the country. Fall arrives with sharp-edged decision, and a luminous sky spreads over Exeter, so that in the crisp clarity of the air the autumn colors stand out sharply. . . . Then, in a month or so, the light goes out of the countryside, the edge of coolness is lost in a general chill, and the look and feel of Exeter dulls. But after Christmas, if it is one of the good old-fashioned winters, a still dry cold crackles around the school, and the ground is clamped beneath a congealed crust covering a foot or more of snow. . . . When spring breaks out, after such a winter, it is plain miracle and it sweeps a whole new way of life into the school."[19] In the last paragraph Knowles draws a parallel between the variety and change in the cycle of the seasons with the boys who also fluctuate and change in these surroundings, coming to a maturity that is rich and lasting as a result of their experiences at this place.

One last piece of ancillary material that forms a part of the creative matrix of *A Separate Peace* is an essay that Knowles wrote for the Yale literary magazine, entitled "A Protest from Paradise."[20] Here he argues that a loss of paradisiacal happiness, such as happened in the summer of 1942 to Gene Forrester and Phineas, may contribute to a writer's attempt to create a fictional image that will make the loss of the actual experience "very much less than complete." He begins the essay with this question: "Are many novels based on the theme of Paradise lost? Are they writers out of a personal sense of longing in the novelist for a real paradise which he once knew, and a real loss he once suffered?" This rhetorical question is answered in the affirmative. He says that writers like Proust, Austen, Tolstoy found themselves in a more perfect world in their youth, where they were entranced by "the sheer joys of living—the weather, people, their own being which made existence seem sublime." Knowles conjectures that, because all of them "possessed strong imaginations and complex apparatuses for responding to the world," this paradisiacal experience "imprinted itself on them with a peculiar force." This magical phase of life eventually ends; something occurs in life to take it away. When this period is gone the author has to confront life as it really is, but the recollections of things past remain and form a permanent assumption of theirs . . . "a feeling about the possibilities of life." Knowles's exposition in *A Separate Peace* is done with realistic accuracy; the scene is recognizable at once to anyone familiar with the grounds of the Phillips Exeter Academy; as one commentator has shown, Knowles made only a few alterations in his fictional adaptation of the prep school backdrop.[21] The three principal sites mentioned in the first chapter are actual places. The Academy Building with its Latin inscription over the portal is in fact the very same as at Exeter, with the exception that the foyer is not marble-floored, although the staircase is. The playing fields and the gym are all very close to the way they were when Knowles was a student in the early 1940s. The actual tree that the boys used to swing from is now gone, but there are others still growing along the bank that would serve the purpose. Knowles altered some facts to heighten the atmospheric effects he wanted to achieve. He mentions, in the article for example, that the river is in reality spanned by a small bridge and that it is not as remote as it seems in the novel from the campus, being only a few hundred yards from the gym and easily reached by a gravel road. Interestingly, Knowles also changed the historical chronology to suit his fictional purpose. The accelerated academic program that allowed boys to finish early by going to summer school did not begin in Exeter until 1943, while at the Devon school it begins in 1942. Perhaps Knowles's purpose was to distance himself from the fictional situations by having his characters one class ahead of his own. Also, by moving up events to 1942, the outcome of the war was not so certain as it would have been a year later, creating a greater sense of anxiety. One senses that in this first novel Knowles was chary of seeming too autobiographical. In the margin of the book's manuscript, he scrawled a note to himself saying that "the narrator is not the writer nor are events in the novel based on events that actually happened." By 1972 he was less reticent about admitting how he specifically adapted real people and events. He revealed in an interview with Phillips Exeter's school newspaper that he projected facets of his own personality into the main characters of *A Separate Peace*. Knowles said that he was not a top student like Gene and had no ambitions to be. Although he could have done better academically, he was not interested in doing any better than was necessary to keep his family, his teachers, and the dean off his back. The character of Phineas was based on a boy named David Hackett who was a regular student at Milton Academy and only attending Exeter for summer session; he was not Knowles's actual roommate, since enrollments in the summer session were so low that boys had single rooms. Finny's

31

natural charm and athletic prowess were inspired by Hackett, but the death of Finny was derived from the case of another Exeter student named Bob Tate, who died on the operating table in the school infirmary on Christmas day when Knowles was a senior, his death the result of a blood clot caused by bone marrow escaping to the brain. Brinker Hadley, a minor character who is the typical "big man on campus" type, was based on another classmate of Knowles's, Gore Vidal, who, Knowles recalled, was an "unusual and thriving" person as a schoolboy, although he did not know him very well.[22] Other characters in the novel were more generic prep school types than specific individuals. For instance, Leper would be a prototypical nonconformist—or "nerd," in today's slang.

Obviously, the genesis of the novel had a profound relationship to the personal life of the author and was grounded in life experiences that have significant meaning to him. Knowles reveals an acute knowledge of certain kinds of people, problems, and issues, and while his experiences and observations are nourished by these special facts, they are given a significance for the world at large.

In an article that Knowles wrote in 1962 entitled "The Young Writer's Real Friends," he describes his mistakes with his first novel, *Descent to Proselito*. He started the novel by outlining its "symbolic pattern" and its "metaphysical paradoxes" but gave up on the advice of Thornton Wilder, because he had begun with symbols before having a story that he was interested in telling or creating people that he really cared about. This led Knowles to write another novel, *A Separate Peace*, about which he says, "if anything as I wrote tempted me to insert artificial complexities, I ignored it. If anything appeared which looked suspiciously like a symbol, I left it on its own. I thought that if I wrote truly and deeply enough about certain specific people in a certain place at a particular time having certain specific experiences, then the result would be relevant for many other kinds of people and places and times and experiences. I know that if I began with symbols, I would end with nothing; if I began with specific individuals, I might end by creating symbols.[23]

There can be little doubt that Knowles wrote *A Separate Peace* with this purpose in mind and following this authorial strategy. Though D. H. Lawrence warns us not to take writers at their word, there is no reason not to think that *A Separate Peace* was the result of Knowles's new approach to fiction. He started with a setting that he knew well, a New England boys' school, and developed episodes and characters taken from his own experiences at that place, thereby constructing a story that communicates with true conviction a concern about a universal human dilemma—the perplexities that attend change and growing up, as we go from the illusions and self-ignorance of childhood to the reality and self-knowledge of adulthood. While being faithful to the physical realities of the persons and places, Knowles transformed his materials, as one critic put it so usefully, into a work of fiction that has "both vitality of verisimilitude and the psychological tension of symbolism."[24]

CHAPTER 5

The Situation

One of Knowles's greatest talents as a writer is his ability to describe scenes and situations. In fact, the appeal of *A Separate Peace* is due in no small part to the way Knowles describes local atmosphere with such clear craftmanship and sure handling of setting as to evoke mood and to advance theme. For example, in the opening section of the novel, which establishes the narrative framework, Knowles's treatment of climate, terrain, and the physical details of the scene, while true to the literal facts he observes, is also highly suggestive of symbolic values.

The narrator, Gene Forrester, begins his story with one of those matter-of-fact statements that open other famous American novels like *Moby Dick* and *The Great Gatsby*. He says, "I went back to the Devon School not long ago, and found it looking oddly newer than when I was a student there fifteen years before" (1). Gene's return to his Devon alma mater is not that of the normal homecoming old graduate. He has not come back to the campus to be reunited with former classmates or to visit with old teachers. Although Gene is now a grown man, he still is haunted, as he tells us, by two fearful places that he wants to see now. He is filled with a sense of anxiety as he returns to the familiar scenes of his boyhood. The unnerving aspect of his experience is underscored in the first paragraph as Gene describes the new—and, to him, disconcerting—aura of sedateness that pervades the campus. It strikes him that the present-day Devon is shinier and more upright than he recalled when he was there during the war years. It is, he says, "as though a coat of varnish had been put over everything for better preservation" (1). The reason Gene is put off by the new impression of the school is that it reminds him of a museum, and although the school buildings now make a better appearance, they are more like relics collected for exhibit, appearing to be different under glass than they were in real life. Gene's emotions at this point are exactly those of anyone who has ever gone back to a place of which he is no longer a part. This attitude is put perfectly by Gene, who reflects, "I had always felt that the Devon School came into existence the day I entered it, was vibrantly real while I was a student there, and then blinked out like a candle the day I left" (1). The return to the campus makes Gene aware of the preservation of something else—fear. Several paragraphs are devoted to a discussion of this unusual revelation. In fact, the reader wonders at this point if Gene is not a criminal returning with great anxiety to the scene of the crime. We assume, at first, that Gene's fears are a result of his having been a schoolboy on the verge of draft age during World War II. It does not appear that the anxiety Gene feels was due to the historical situation, however, because the fearful sites that he has in mind are a building and a tree. He has come back to confront the fear that these places instilled in him and to see if he has made his escape from it.

In keeping with the grim purpose that has brought him back to Devon, the weather is a raw, late November day, a fittingly appropriate wet, "self-pitying" kind of winter day with the wind blowing in "moody gusts" all around and "stripped, moaning trees" (2). Gene soon locates the first place he seeks—the First Academy Building, a Georgian-style red brick structure with an inscription in Latin over the doorway that reads *Hic venite pueri et viri sitis*. The appearance of the Academy Building strikes Gene as being essentially the same as he remembered. Entering through the swinging doors into a marble-

The First Academy Building at Exeter. The Latin inscription over the portal reads: "Here come boys to be made into men."
Photograph by Hallman Bell Bryant.

floored foyer, Gene reveals to the reader what he has come to see—"a long white marble flight of stairs." The steps do not go up to an old dormitory room as we might expect; in fact, all we are told about the stairs concerns their hardness, "a crucial fact" that had been previously overlooked. The reader does not have enough information to comprehend the irony of this remark or to understand why Gene would choose to look at these steps in the first place. But we later discover that an event that deeply influenced his life took place here. Fifteen years before, Gene had been brought here by a group of Devon schoolmates to be accused of causing an accident that crippled his roommate, and on these stairs another accident happened that killed his best friend.

The Situation

As Gene confronts this place that witnessed such tragic events, he remarks on how little the scene has changed: "There was nothing else to notice; they of course were the same stairs I had walked up and down at least once every day of my Devon life. They were the same as ever. And I? Well, I naturally felt older—I began at that point the emotional examination to note how far my convalescence had gone—I was taller, bigger generally in relation to these stairs" (3).

Although we are told little about the narrator at this point—where he has come from, what he does for a living, or even his name—we sense there is something compulsive about the reason for his return. Gene's tone is often ironic as he measures himself against the events of a time in his past fifteen years before, but it indicates that his purpose in coming back to Devon is to make a judgment upon himself. By extension, Knowles is controlling our responses to Gene. He shows that Gene has arrived at a state of material as well as moral maturity; he is unwilling to excuse his former actions and is now ready to accept full responsibility for what has happened. He is thus taller, bigger and more secure "than in the days when specters seemed to go up and down them [stairs] with me" (3).

Knowles's ability to evoke a parallel between persons and places is revealed as the scene shifts back outdoors with Gene seeking out the other "fearful site." The final test of his development will be his confrontation with the second place he had come to see. Looking across the school grounds, he notes that there is a beauty about the place that derives from "areas of order" comprising arrangements of trees, dormitories, quadrangles and houses in small groupings of "contentious harmony." This observation leads Gene to reflect on the paradoxical way that the new and old are reconciled: "Everything at Devon slowly changed and slowly harmonized with what had gone before" (4), and if such adjustments are possible for institutions, he concludes that it is logical for him to hope that the individual can find a similar balance: "I could achieve, perhaps unknowingly already had achieved, this growth and harmony myself" (4).

With this expectation before him, the narrator makes his way past the school gymnasium, now standing "silent as a monument," and past the Field House, suggestively called "The Cage"—a name that recalls for Gene, with its connotations of mystery and lurking bestiality, how much of his earlier experience at Devon had been full of anxiety. Making his way across the soft, muddy ground of the vast playing fields, the narrator reveals what the purpose of the quest is— "to look at a tree" (5).

The progression across the athletic field is described in terms of unpleasant images that define the distaste that Gene feels for the place he is approaching. The mud "dooms" his dress shoes, the choice of word here suggesting that it is his destiny to return to the tree, despite the damage done to his shoes. Further, there is an "obscene" sucking noise made by his feet as he pulls them out of the mire, which heightens the sense of aversion.

The size of the playing fields has added meaning here. Their size seems exaggerated, and to cross them requires a long walk over "enormous, endless green playing fields." The vastness of the scene makes it seem lonelier and creates a greater degree of mystery about Gene's guilt.

It is important to note at this point that all the elements seem to conspire to defeat Gene's purpose. The wind flings wet gusts of rain, and the fog over the river thickens as if to frustrate and confuse him. He confesses that at any other time he would have felt like a fool slogging through mud, rain, and mist to find a tree. Of course, each of these facts of weather can be seen as symbolic. The mud that clings to Gene's shoes recalls the mud at the bottom of the river that he sinks into after leaping from the tree. Thus, the mud that is so disgusting in sight and sound suggests a return to something elemental, a primal emotion linked with fear and revulsion. The rain likewise has a larger implication; as in Hemingway's *A Farewell to Arms,* it is a bitter rather than a refreshing rain that defines the unpleasant reality of things. In addition, a fog hangs over the river, obscuring his way and making his task of reorientation even more difficult, perhaps an indication that his vision of the past has been affected by the passage of time. The fog also isolates Gene, cutting him off from everything except the river and the tree—the two memories with which he still has to come to terms. Portentously, the wind grows colder and Gene feels a chill, as if the ghosts that had haunted his youth are still about.

At first Gene is confused by the fact that all trees he now sees along the river appear to be so much alike. "Any one of them might have been the one I was looking for" (5). The important thing to understand here is that, although there may have been physical changes in trees, the most important change has been psychological, and it has taken place within the mind of the narrator. In maturity, his perspective on the world is totally different from what it had been in youth. For instance, he says that the tree "had loomed in my memory as a huge lone spike dominating the riverbank, forbidding as an artillery piece, high as the beanstalk" (5). Each simile evokes an image of the tree as it once appeared to Gene, posing an element of threat and danger. It is equated with a spike that is intimidating because of its height, a large gun whose huge barrel threatens, and the magic beanstalk, a forbidden place in folklore that leads to the presence of a terrible giant.

Where the tree in Gene's imagination had loomed large and intimidating, its size, color, and shape exaggerated, it now appears like all the other trees. After a close examination of several of the trees by the river, "his" tree is finally identified by means of small nail marks that have left scars on the trunk. In his choice of words, Gene may on one level be subconsciously equating the scars on the tree with the scars that marked his own psyche in his youth, which he fears to reopen. However, the tree appears diminished just as the staircase did—a double demotion has taken place. The tree has "grown weary from age, enfeebled, dry," while Gene, it is implied, has grown; the tree appears to him like "those men, the giants of your childhood, whom you encounter years later and find that they are not merely smaller in relation to your growth, but that they are absolutely smaller, shrunken by age" (6).

The reaction to the changes in the physical appearance of the two sites the narrator has returned to see mirrors his own psychological change. Change, it occurs to him, is a part of the general design of things, and in his case he is heartened by this because if nothing remains the same, "not a tree, not love, not even a death by violence," then there is hope that he has been altered as well. In fact, he feels that his pilgrimage back to Devon has confirmed that hope for him: "Changed, I headed back through the mud. I was drenched; anybody could see it was time to come in out of the rain" (6). Again the choice of physical details points to a symbolic meaning. The water images suggest that something has been washed away, that a stain has been removed. Gene, his ordeal over, can now face himself and the consequences of his past actions. So, "changed," he comes back in out of the rain, freed from the fears these two scenes once had for him.

CHAPTER 6

Before the Fall

In the narrative that follows Gene's visits to the stairs and the tree, time reverts to the summer of 1942, the first year of World War II, when Gene stood with Phineas, his roommate, and three other classmates on the same spot by the riverbank. Appropriately, the action begins where the narrative prologue leaves off, beneath the tree. As we have seen in our reading so far, one of Gene's motives in returning to Devon is to determine how far he has come in fifteen years in his attempt to escape the fears of his youth, when, "like stale air in an unopened room was the well-known fear which had surrounded and filled those days, so much of it that I hadn't even known it was there" (1). At this point the reader dramatically discovers the exact source of this fear, and we are, like Gene, confronted with it—the tree. The shift from one narrative perspective to another is intentionally obvious; Gene the thirty-three-year-old man sees the tree as "weary from age, enfeebled, dry . . . :" beginning with the middle paragraph on page six, however, Gene the sixteen-year-old boy perceives the tree, which is used by the upperclassmen as part of their wartime program of physical training, as a "tremendous, irate, steely, black steeple. . . . " The situation that unfolds begins in *medias res* with Gene, characteristically, in an uncomfortable position. He has just been challenged by Phineas, his roommate, to climb the tree, but he thinks to himself: "I was damned if I'd climb it. The hell with it. No one but Phineas could think up such a crazy idea" (6). This is a new narrative voice that will be used for the rest of the novel except for a few occasions, which will be noted. The line between the adult and the adolescent narrator is practically indistinct. As one commentator, Ian Kennedy, says of the point of view in the novel, Knowles constructs his narrative so that we are often misled by Gene's youthful misconceptions and kept unaware of a proper recognition of the facts so that "we can share the intensity of his misguided feelings."[25]

In this very first episode of the novel, a number of revealing traits about Gene are brought out, the most obvious being his sense of resentment against his friend. Not only has Phineas dared to put him on the spot, but his blasé attitude about undertaking such a perilous feat puts Gene off. Furthermore, the sound of his voice and his appearance in general annoy him. Phineas's green eyes are wide and maniacal-looking, and only his smirking mouth makes Gene know that "he wasn't completely goofy" (6). Gene's defense against Phineas's ingeniousness is sarcasm. Although there is no judgment passed on this trait, there is a sense of distance in the remark " . . . that was my sarcastic summer, 1942." It is not likely that Gene at this moment would have the perspective to see this stage in his life as sarcastic—with the implied recognition that there was something defective about such a response to life. "It was only long after that I recognized sarcasm as the protest of people who are weak" (22). The shift from one narrative perspective to the other is rarely so obvious; it is usually the boy's voice that narrates what happens in the novel and the adult's voice that interprets the events, as in the situation above.

Gene resents Finny because of his naturally confident attitude, his easy physical courage that causes him to think that leaping from such a high tree would be a "cinch." To Gene, however, the tree is threatening (a soaring black spire with its steeplelike trunk). He would be "damned" if he would climb it, and he dismissed Finny's idea with a contemptuous remark, saying, "the hell with it." Gene's actions in this very first scene show certain characteristic negative traits: his fear of not measuring up in the eyes of his peer group, his latent hostility toward and envy of Finny, and his tendency to use indirect responses such as sarcasm in verbal retaliation. He is envious of Finny's courage, his athletic prowess, and in particular his powers of persuasion—a capacity that resides in his hypnotic voice. Against such a compelling personality, Gene knows that he and the three other boys on this occasion will be finagled into doing what Finny wants. All except Finny are inhibited by the danger; undaunted, he climbs the tree effortlessly, none of the other boys having accepted his invitation to go first.

At this point Finny is described for us in more detail. Gene notes that Finny is the best athlete in the school, yet he is not especially large. In fact, he and Gene are nearly the same in size. The two boys are both five feet, eight-and-one-half inches tall, although Gene had claimed to be five feet, nine inches until Finny forced him to acknowledge the truth about himself. However, Finny at 155 pounds weighs a "crucial five pounds more" than Gene. Here again we are given what initially seem to be routine facts, which will later turn out to be significant. Gene and Finny are very similar physically, but the psychological difference between them is vast, the major difference being that Gene lacks the security and confidence of his roommate. His basic insecurity is revealed in his lie about the one-half inch difference in height; we see Gene intent on gaining even even this slight an advance over Finny, whom he obviously thinks of in terms of rivalry. The five pounds of weight that Finny has on Gene is a fact filled with implications. As we will see later on, Finny is a "larger" person than Gene in terms of spirit; he has a greater heart and more magnanimity, which would symbolically account for this greater weight. Always the master of understatement, Knowles describes small details such as the peculiar inflictions of pronunciation that make Finny remarkable. His way of saying yes by using a "weird New England affirmative" is noted. Finny always says "aey-rh," which makes Gene laugh. This small mannerism is in itself not very important, but taken in the total context of the boys' relationship, it shows that Finny knows he can influence Gene, in this case by amusing him.

With his resistance broken down by Finny's comic manners, Gene accepts the dare, climbs the tree against his better judgment and, following Finny's example, leaps into the river. This is the most significant piece of action of the opening chapter, and, appropriately, it is an episode in which the central characters are vying with each other. This episode mirrors the basic conflict of the novel: the alternating feelings of hostility and compatibility that Gene has for Phineas, combined with Gene's feeling that he is "throwing his life away" by doing Finny's bidding. On the other hand, his bold but illegal act—the tree was out of bounds to the juniors—makes Gene feel a sense of cohesiveness with Finny that momentarily liberates Gene. Summoned by the dinner bell, the boys then start back toward the school, already late for the meal. Gene experiences a sense of "behavior modification," feeling that he is best friends with Finny for the moment; he assumes Finny's attitudes and point of view. "I suddenly became his collaborator. As we walked along, I abruptly resented the bell and my West Point stride and hurrying and conforming. Finny was right" (11).

In the exchange of dialogue between Finny and Gene at this point, Knowles drops hints of some of Gene's most telling limitations and of Finny's most basic virtues. For example, Gene is chided by Finny because he had to shame him into jumping, adding that Gene has "a tendency to back away from things," a charge that Gene resents because he knows that it is true. Gene's stiff, formal manner is indicated by his body language, his "West Point stride," which is in contrast to Finny's serene walk that "flowed on, rolling forward . . . with such unthinking unity of movement that 'walk' didn't describe it"(10). It is important to understand that Finny has intuitively comprehended qualities in Gene that he wants to alter, especially his tendency to play by the rules and to toady to authority. Finny considers "authority the necessary evil against which happiness was achieved by reaction, the backboard which returned all the insults he threw at it" (11). Thus, Gene's fast-paced, precise military way of walking is intolerable to Finny and he trips him up, throwing him down in the grass. After a brief wrestling match, the boys hurry to try to get back on time, but Gene, as if to show that he has subscribed to Finny's tendency to flaunt the rules, uncharacteristically trips up Finny, who is delighted by this trick since he likes surprises and unexpected situations where he is not totally in control. There is, of course, a great deal of latent irony in this particular situation, which foreshadows Gene's subsequent trick on Finny that will result in the unexpected fall that cripples him.

The action of the chapter closes out with dinner being missed and the two boys returning to their room. Knowles has, however, suggested a multiplicity of meanings in this short episode. The carefully selected descriptive details are endowed with significances that the reader will not realize until later, as the themes and characterizations come into sharper focus. For example, one of the novel's themes is Gene's gradual self-understanding, and even his initial responses to Finny are full of portent; the smallest gestures can be seen as harbingers of the ultimate outcome. In the moment after Gene has jumped from the tree at Finny's behest, he emerges from the water as if from a baptism, although that term is not used by Knowles. In the afterglow of pride from having done a brave thing, Gene's whole state of consciousness is raised. The grass appears greener, more fragrant, and more nourished by the just-risen dews of evening. In this serene twilight there are numerous sounds that Gene's ears, having been "rinsed" by his experience, seem to register with amazing acuteness. " . . . now I could hear cricket noises and bird cries of dusk, a gymnasium truck gunning along an empty athletic road a quarter of a mile away, a burst of faint, isolated laughter carried to us from the back door of the gym, and then over all, cool and matriarchal, the six o'clock bell from the Academy Building cupola, the calmest, most carrying bell toll in the world, civilized, calm, invincible, and final" (10). The heightened auditory sense that predominates in the final lines of this scene serves several purposes. Most importantly, the refinement of Gene's hearing makes him more like Finny, who has "extrasensory ears"—a boy whose hearing is so sharp that it seems more like intuition than a mere sensory faculty and who can "feel in the air someone coming on him from behind" (11)—which further strengthens the momentary bonding between the two boys. Finny's almost miraculous senses will, however, later fail to alert him of danger at a crucial moment; he will not sense peril in time to save himself from Gene's treachery.

The first chapter closes with an evocative description of the Devon campus that could only have been drawn from "a spot of time," as Wordsworth called those stored memories that are accumulated and recycled through our imagination, becoming something finer and more precious than the actual experience. Here the writing becomes suggestive of larger meanings, especially the allusions to the titles of several popular songs and classical music that drift out from a phonograph playing in a dormitory, as the boys make their way back to their room. It has been pointed out by previous commentators that there is considerable irony in the fact that the first song heard is "Don't Sit Under the Apple Tree," a cautionary wartime tune admonishing a girl not to betray her boyfriend while he is away in the service; in both cases the tree is associated with something forbidden, and a betrayal of trust is implied. The connection between events in the novel and the title of the second song is perhaps more tenuous, but "They're Either Too Young or Too Old" seems to anticipate the theme of youth and the generation gap created by the war. It is interesting to note that both songs deal with wartime frustrations, the first revealing the man's anxiety about the loyalty of his girlfriend and the second voicing a girl's complaint that all the men left back home in wartime are the wrong age. The third piece of music mentioned is "The Warsaw Concerto," which also ties in with the war theme and foreshadows the claim made by Finny in the next chapter that the allies have bombed central Europe. Finally, the last piece is "The Nutcracker Suite," which points toward another motif that appears later—the theme of insanity. Leper, a classmate, has a nervous breakdown in basic training, literally becoming "nutty," and Gene himself struggles at another critical point in the novel to keep his own sanity.

A further detail that should be noted is that the boys are reading two Hardy novels as an English assignment. Gene's book is *Tess of the d'Urbervilles,* a novel about a guilt-striken heroine who can never escape the consequences of an impetuous act. Finny, on the other hand, is reading *Far From the Madding Crowd,* one of Hardy's few novels with a positive outcome. The protagonist is the naturally decent Gabriel Oak, a man of great natural virtues—very much like Finny.

Chapter 2 begins with an exchange between Finny and one of the substitute teachers, Mr. Prud'homme, who questions Finny about breaking the rule about attending evening meals. The excuse that Finny gives is so bizarre that the man is more amused than angry: he tells Mr. Prud'homme that it was more important to jump out of the tree as a part of the war effort than to come in for dinner. Mr. Prud'homme is no less amazed by Finny's candor and friendliness than by the scatterbrained response, so he laughs at the boy rather than reprobating him. Gene senses that this tolerance is caused by wartime. "I think we reminded them of what peace was like, we boys of sixteen. We were registered with no draft board, we had taken no physical examinations. . . . I suppose we could be thought of as a sign of the life the war was being fought to preserve. . . . We reminded them of what peace was like, of lives which were not bound up with destruction" (17).

Gene also sees that Finny is the "essence of this careless peace," that it is due to his unique personality as well as the times that the faculty has taken a more lenient stance. They had never encountered a boy like Finny who combined a disregard for the rules with a desire to be good, who seemed to sincerely love the school yet flaunt its regulations, so they threw up their hands over his case and thus "loosened their grip" on the other students.

The scene at the tea party given by Mr. Patch-Withers provides additional insights into the relaxed conditions at the school and reveals that Gene is developing a tincture of envy towards Finny. To this very stiff and formal occasion, Finny has the effrontery to wear a pink shirt. In an earlier time, before school dress codes had become as relaxed as they are now, such an item of apparel would have indeed been shocking.

It might be useful to examine at this juncture the significance of this shirt as a symbol of Finny's personality and as a device to suggest the cultural and historical ambience of the period. The use of an item of clothing as a signature of a character's essential nature is prevalent in American literature. One thinks of the pink ribbons worn by the wife of young Goodman Brown in Hawthorne's short story and the extravagant pink suit that Jay Gatsby wore to impress Daisy in Fitgerald's *The Great Gatsby*. Although wearing a pink shirt in 1942 was not as outrageous as wearing a pink suit in high society during the 1920s, it was nevertheless an audacious thing to do. If, as Gene says, the prevailing color of the 1940s was olive green, in civilian dress shirts it was still white. In men's clothing at the time, colored dress shirts were regarded as radical fashion items. Finny's shirt has the characteristics of a classic Brooks Brothers model, which was a historic shirt. Introduced in 1940, it was the first pink shirt for men, breaking a long tradition of using only white in dress shirts.[26] It is made of "a finely woven broad cloth that is carefully cut and very pink," with a high collar, and a yoke-neck which appeals to Finny very much "because it is unusual." He says to Gene, "Did you ever see stuff like this, and a color like this? It doesn't even button all the way down. You have to pull it over your head . . ." (17).

The unique features of this shirt do not go unnoticed by the conservative-natured Gene, who asks Finny as he takes his proud possession (which his mother had bought for him) out of the drawer, "What's that thing?"—adding sarcastically that the pink shirt "makes you look like a fairy." But Finny is undaunted by taunts, surer of himself and his sexuality than Gene, and he is not troubled in the least by the imputation that he will appear effeminate. In fact, he seems mildly amused that he might appear as a homosexual to his classmates and speculates what would happen if "suitors begin clamoring at the door" (18).

Finny, however, does not don the shirt as a declaration of his sexual preference; he claims that he is wearing the shirt "as an emblem" which he will use in lieu of a flag since they "can't float Old Glory proudly out the window" (18). Finny does indeed wear his pink shirt proudly, "something no one else in the school could have done without some risk of having it torn from his back." The shirt becomes a talisman for Finny during the course of the day that he wears it. In his classes he disarms the the teachers who critically inquire about his unusually colored shirt. Even the stern history instructor, old Mr. Patch-Withers, is diverted by Finny's explanation, and his drawn pink face becomes pinker with amusement when Finny tells him the meaning of the shirt.

During the afternoon Finny pushes his luck even further and combines the shirt with the Devon school tie, which he wears as a belt. This is the third time during the day that Finny has been in a tentative situation, and again, much to Gene's chagrin, he is able to talk himself out of it. Although the Hollywood star Fred Astaire had begun the fad of putting a tie through his belt loops to hold trousers, it was a small act of impiety on Finny's part to use the school tie in such a fashion, indicating as it did a lack of respect for the traditions the tie stood for. The headmaster's wife is aghast when she sees him wearing the official tie for a belt, but Finny's mind is as agile as Huckleberry Finn's when it comes to making up a lie on the spur of the moment, and he accounts for himself easily with a patriotic alibi. He claims that the tie and shirt all go together—they "tie in" with the successful allied bombing raid on central Europe and are thus symbolic of how the school is "involved in everything that happens in the war . . ." (20). Finny's logic involves such an extreme *non sequitur* that the faculty are amused rather than indignant and Finny again escapes censure.

This episode reveals, as does the scene with Mr. Prud'homme, that the war has changed the norms of the school; conventional reactions are in abeyance, giving a nonconformist like Finny more latitude. Both scenes give greater insight into the characters of Gene and Finny as well as providing richer context for the enveloping action. In each case Finny's reasons for his actions have to do with the war effort. In the case of the jump out of the tree he was getting ready for combat, and in wearing the pink shirt and school tie he was manifesting a "war attitude," an attitude encouraged in all Americans by no less than FDR.

The adult attitude toward the war is succinctly revealed in the chitchat about the air raid. One of the faculty wives agrees with Finny that the bombers should not hit women, children, or old people and should avoid hospitals, schools, and churches. She is especially concerned that works of art of "permanent value" be spared. Her husband voices a realistic view of such naive expectations by saying it would be impossible to bomb with such precision and adds condescendingly that, besides, there isn't any "permanent art" in central Europe.

Although the bombing raid on central Europe that so excites Finny was probably one of his spontaneous prevarications (since no such raids were made until 1943 when the U.S. Army Air Force attacked the Ploesti oil fields), there was justification for the elation at the news, because in 1942 the United States and the other Allies have very little to cheer about. Most of the U.S. Navy had been sunk at Pearl Harbor, and the U.S. Army had surrendered the largest number of troops in history to the Japanese on Bataan in the Philippines. Thus, lacking any real good news to raise morale, the exuberant Finny makes up some for the occasion.

Although Gene's admiration and affection for Finny are evident at this point, a countercurrent of resentment and jealousy is building up in Gene. He envies Finny's special knack for breaking the rules and getting away with it. "I couldn't help envying him that a little . . ." (18), he admits, and adds ironically, ". . . which was perfectly normal. There was no harm in envying even your best friend a little" (18). Gene's resentment takes the form of a covert desire to see his friend fail to bring off one of his verbal charades. He thinks during Finny's escapade at the tea that "he wasn't going to get away with it," and he begins to anticipate Finny's failure excitedly. When Finny talks his way out the breach of decorum with the tie, Gene feels a "stab of disappointment." He tells himself that it was only because he wants to see more excitement, but the reader should see that Gene's callous justification is a sign of self-ignorance and his desire for Finny's failure pure vindictiveness. He really wants to see Finny get into a difficult situation that he can't get out of. However, he knows that Finny likes nothing more than to put himself in predicaments, to do the unexpected thing, or to say something so illogical that no one can argue with him. These traits, like playing games, jumping out of trees, or defying authority, are basically childish. Gene, on the other hand, is trying to become an adult and to live in accord with the expectations of the grown-up world; his ambivalent attitude toward Finny, therefore, is to some extent caused by his conflicting desire to remain a juvenile. Knowles, like all good writers, is, at this stage of his characters' development, exploring the nature and meaning of their actions and establishing the basic situation of conflict between Gene and Finny. At this point, however, the conflict is largely nascent; it exists mostly in Gene's own mind. Concealed even from himself, Gene covets those qualities of Finny that he most lacks—a spontaneous and imaginative response to life, along with the courage to abide by his own principles rather than by rules imposed by others.

Gene's cautious, competitive nature is the antithesis of Finny's, yet for some time during the idyllic weeks of midsummer he is content to accept Finny's proposals, even when it comes to making a dangerous double jump out of the tree to cap the victory he has won by making the headmaster laugh about the tie incident. The double jump is proposed as a sign of their partnership, and, to give it more significance, Finny requires the seal of a formal name. Thus is born the "Super Suicide Society," membership being contingent upon making a leap out of the tree. Right now it is a very select society, since only Gene and Finny belong. The selection of this name is certainly appropriate, given the hazardous nature of the jump, which is brought out by Gene's near-fatal slip when he panics on the limb and almost loses his balance. Finny is there to save him from falling, however, and he makes a safe leap.

Reflecting later on the incident, Gene realizes what a close call he had and that, had Finny not been there, he could have been killed. In a sense then, what he was doing was suicidal indeed, but even more self-destructive was his giving in to Finny's whimsical notions, leading Gene to believe that he is throwing away his life by following Finny's example.

Nowhere is the sense of an Edenic existence brought out better than in some of the descriptive passages in this part of the book. In such idyllic terrain and climate the war seems totally unreal. Neither Gene nor Finny can imagine bombs falling anywhere. The ivy-covered dormitories give the impression of the hanging gardens of the Bible transported to America. The campus elms soar heavenward, lofty complexes of branches, "a world of branches with an infinity of leaves. They too seemed permanent and never-changing, an untouched, unreachable world high in space, like ornamental towers and spires of a great church . . ."(23). The arboreal images define quite clearly the conception of the demiparadise in which boys dwelt for a brief time. Trees also figure as symbols in this passage when Gene meditates on the woods that lie beyond the athletic fields. In his imagination the trees were the beginning of the great northern forests, which reached in an "unbroken, widening corridor so far to the north that no one had ever seen the other end, somewhere up in the far unorganized tips of Canada" (23). Gene is here depicted as an American Adam, "playing on the fringe of the last and greatest wilderness" (23), and, as the heightening of language suggests, the forest image stands for some great, good place that is the last frontier of innocence.

In Chapter 3 the countertension between admiration and abhorrence for Finny is further developed. The ambivalence of Gene's attitude is revealed in three episodes. The first is the invention of a new game by Finny; the second occurs when Finny breaks a school swimming record and refuses to repeat or report the accomplishment; the third involves cutting classes to travel to the nearby beaches.

In addition to the nocturnal activities of the secret Super Suicide Society, which meets every night to induct new members, Finny comes up with an invented game for the daytime called blitzball. Typically, the creation of this sport was the result of Finny's rebellion against the school's established summer athletic program. He is especially disdainful of badminton because it is too refined and not played with a ball, which to him is a necessity for any decent sports contest. Ironically, this game becomes the most popular form of recreation during the idyllic summer session—ironically because it takes its very name from the newsreels and headlines of the period that proclaimed a new kind of war—blitzkreig, or "lightning war," as Germany's savagely efficient form of total war was called. The game is a grim reminder of the real war going on in the world beyond the playing fields. In keeping with the war motif, the players in the game are called "enemies." There are no predetermined sides, and the point of the game is to "blitz" or wipe out whoever is carrying the ball at the moment. The only way for the ball carrier to avoid being tackled is to pass the ball off to someone else. It is important to note that Finny's athletic creations involve no premeditation; the rules for blitzball are made up *ad hoc* in the very heat of the game. For example, when the ball is passed off to the timid Lepellier, he refuses to accept it, so Finny comes up on the spot with a rule to cover the situation: the so-called "Lepellier Refusal," which permits a player to refuse the pass if he chooses. Another small but significant detail concerning the game is the manner in which it is played. Although the principles of the game are essentially brutal, involving little more than physically overpowering the competition, there are opportunities for gifted players to excel. Gene observes that the game brought Finny's athletic powers to their fullest potential, especially when he carried the ball—the odds were against him, but it is exactly because he is disadvantaged that he was driven to exceed himself. "To escape the wolf pack which all the other players became he created reverses annd deceptions and acts of sheer mass hypnotism which were so extraordinary that they surprised even him . . ." (31). One should keep in mind that Finny's conflict exists only on the athletic field, and, as Gene comes to realize later, Finny is "a poor deceiver, having had no practice." In the world of sports, as Finny aphoristically puts it, "you always win. . . . Everyone always won at sports. . . . Nothing bad ever happened in sports; they were the absolute good" (26–27). Thus, Finny's innocent game invented to add zest to the summer sports scene is more than just an example of his zany spontaneity; it is a symbol of his innermost nature and also a reflection of the realities of the period of the Second World War, where nations practice diplomatic deceptions and blitz with bombs instead of balls.

Another sporting experience that shows Finny's devotion to athletics for purposes of pure enjoyment rather than ego gratification is his breaking of the school's 100-meter swimming record. In a characteristically impetuous move, Finny decides, without any practice, to challenge the record just for the fun of it, and he succeeds in breaking it by

.07 of a second. His response to his triumph is unique; he refuses to report his feat and pledges Gene to silence. Gene is astonished at Finny's attitude. His reaction is to call attention to victory and to make sure it is official so that due credit for the accomplishment will be given. He is both dazzled and amazed by the turn of events and also a bit suspicious that Finny is trying to dupe or impress him by refusing to claim the record.

Although Gene's admiration of Finny is largely unqualified, he covets Finny's charisma and fears that he can never measure up to his natural physical superiority. Furthermore, he is apprehensive that Finny is gaining a Svengali-like influence over him, making him a passive partner in a relationship that is growing more tormented for him.

Gene's frustration is brought out in the episode where Finny convinces Gene to cut class one day in late August so that they can spend an afternoon at the nearby seashore. Gene is reluctant to go because of an important math exam the next day, but he cannot resist Finny's "hypnotic" powers of persuasion and puts his status as a Devon student at risk. The trip to the ocean, which climaxes the period of innocence, is one of the most telling of the early scenes in the novel, and, if the relevant details are read carefully, they shed light on the novel's emerging ideas and themes. For example, arriving at the beach after a three-hour bicycle ride, Finny frolics in the waves for an entire hour before he has his fill of the surging sea's force, whereas Gene, reluctant as always to risk himself for no reason, comes out of the dangerous surf after only a few moments of being battered by the undertow. Finny, previously described as having prow-shaped facial features and whose nickname suggests his fishlike attributes, seems to have found his true element. The wild, untamed sea is a force that cannot be regulated; Finny's affinity with the ocean shows a kinship with nature that complements his own spirit, and which might best be described in the high romantic terms of Shelley: "tameless, swift and proud." In fact, it should be noticed that Finny's very nature seems enhanced by the sunshine, the ocean, and the "salty, adventurous, flirting wind from the sea." Gene senses that the influence of nature has an intoxicating effect on Finny; people were staring at him because his tan skin is radiating with a "reddish-copper glow" and by contrast his eyes shine with "a cool blue-green fire" (39). Finny's exceptional appearance indicates his close communion with nature and underscores a theme of romanticism that runs through the novel: the belief that our greatest happiness comes from a life lived near primitive, natural forces. It seems clear that, in the beach episode, Knowles is drawing an analogy between Finny and the romantic concept of the child of nature. The chromatic images of red, blue, and green endow Finny with an almost religious aura, cloaked as he is in a nimbus of natural light that breaks from his body and eyes. He is totally "turned on" by his experiences and aglow with some miraculous light.

Gene, dressed in his white T-shirt and ducks, is a colorless contrast to the vibrant Finny. His preoccupation with breaking rules and with returning to school in time to take his math test prevents him from fully participating in the forces of the natural world that Finny is so in harmony with, especially now, near ocean waters. Having prevented him from falling from the tree, Gene resents Finny for being the cause of putting him in such a dangerous situation to begin with; rather than admiring Finny's humility in not broadcasting his swimming feat, Gene is puzzled and overawed, thinking there is something so unnatural about Finny that he cannot be regarded as a rival. Even Finny's candid admission to Gene at the beach that he is his "best pal" fails to relieve his reservations; he does not reply in kind as he knows he should. Gene is only appearing at this point to be a friend; he is too self-centered to express true friendship.

Thus far the plot has moved through an ascending series of scenes that revealed complications or tension, but Knowles is building up to the "defining event" of the novel, the major complications of the story, the point where the basis of the conflict is illuminated most fully.

The opening lines of Chapter 4 describe the coming of dawn at the seashore, a new experience for Gene, who has never seen a sunrise. Here, we are presented with an event that is treated in a clearly symbolic manner. The dominant impression at first is that everything appears to be dead. Finny sleeping seems to Gene to be more dead than asleep; the ocean looks gray and deathlike. The sky seems encased in a gray burlap, giving Gene the feeling of being closed in. Gradually this spectral scene is transformed as the sunrise brings light and color to the sky and sea. Not since Stephen Crane's short story "The Open Boat" has a seascape been executed so graphically by an American writer. Knowles compares the gathering dawn to an orchestra tuning up: "Very gradually, like one instrument after another being tentatively rehearsed, beacons of color began to piece the sky. The ocean perked up a little from the reflection of these colored slivers in the sky. Bright high lights shone on the tips of the waves, and beneath its gray surface I could see lurking a deep midnight green" (41). The beach is transformed before Gene's eyes from something grim and ghostly into a scene "totally white and stainless, as pure as the shores of Eden." In the midst of this radiance the sleeping Phineas reminds Gene of Lazarus, the biblical character who was brought back from the dead by Jesus. The implications of the sunrise and the association of it with scripture ironically do not make themselves felt on Gene, who admits, "I didn't contemplate this transformation for long" (41). He moves to measured manmade clock time rather than the rhythms of nature's time, driven "by a sense of time ticking steadily." It is totally in keeping with Gene's commitment to schedules, routines, and ambitious agendas that he would be controlled by the artificial measuring of time. On the other hand, Finny exists outside of regulated time, heedless of anything except the present moment. Thus, Gene's sleep was broken by his biological clock that told him it was six o'clock while Finny sleeps on without a care, finally rousing to declare that the night on the dunes was the best sleep he ever had. In an ominous bit of foreshadowing, Gene asks Finny if he ever had a bad sleep, to which he replies that he once did when he broke his ankle. In light of subsequent events this fact seems ominous, but there are other aspects of this scene that could be taken as foreshadowing. For instance, the use of biblical images seems indicative of a number of later developments. As the landscape is transformed from a moribund state, so Lazarus was reanimated by Christ. Likewise, Finny will eventually die, but through the example of his life Gene will be transformed.

Just as Gene had feared, the expedition to the beach causes him to fail his test. It is a mortifying experience for him because it is the first failing grade of his student career. Gene attributes his academic disaster to Finny's influence, which he begins to try to analyze. He comes to the conclusion that Finny's motive is a jealous desire to wreck Gene's chances to become the top student academically. He suspects that Finny's purpose is to make him into an obedient disciple who will jump out of trees or run off from school. Of course, these perceptions are entirely mistaken. His rationalizations have led him to a false conclusion. One reason for the ambiguity surrounding Gene's motivations and actions at this juncture is the discrepancy between Gene's judgments and the actions and attitudes he is evaluating. Because the narration is restricted to the point of view of the younger Gene, his interpretation of Finny's actions is distorted by his uncertainties about his friend, which have been building up, as we have seen, ever since the episode at the gym where Finny's refusal to take credit for his swimming accomplishment takes root in Gene's mind and "grew rapidly in the darkness where I was forced to hide it" (36). At the beach Finny's frank declaration of friendship troubles Gene and his response was "stopped by that level of feeling, deeper than thought, which contains the truth" (40). These inchoate intuitions congeal into an idea that causes Gene to conclude that he should reject Finny as a friend. He now understands that Phineas is his rival and deduces that their relationship has been regulated all along by envy and enmity.

In a moment of erroneous insight, Gene says to himself, "I found it. I found a single sustaining thought . . . enmity. You are both coldly driving ahead for yourselves alone. You did hate him for breaking that school swimming record, but so what? He hated you for getting an A in every course but one last term" (45).

Although the reader cannot be sure of the validity of Gene's assumptions now, it will be apparent later that the vices that Gene attributes to Finny are projections of his own personality and are feelings entirely absent from Finny's heart. The unreality of Gene's analysis is revealed through the subsequent action in this chapter, which is structured so that the interpretation of motive is provided by the adult Gene rather than the adolescent.

Having determined that their relationship is grounded on mutual hatred, everything for the moment is clear and Gene feels a sense of relief. He can now comprehend his reactions to Finny at the tea party, the gym, and the beach where his admiration was tinged with antagonism. "I felt better. We were even after all, even in enmity. The deadly rivalry was on both sides after all" (46). Gene thinks that he has a good chance of outclassing Finny in this head-to-head rivalry and believes himself at the moment to be his peer: "I was more and more certainly becoming the best student in the school; Phineas was without question the best athlete, so in a way we were even. But while he was a very poor student, I was a pretty good athlete, and when everything was thrown into the scales they would in the end tilt definitely toward me" (47).

Although Gene's announced ambition, at least to himself, is to be head of the class on graduation day and win the Ne Plus Ultra prize for scholarship, he is not intrinsically a scholar—as he well knows when he compares himself with another bright student, Chet Douglas, who is a true intellectual and honestly excited by learning, someone who follows knowledge for its own sake. In fact, Gene, who is more interested in grades than any final wisdom he might gain from a course, sees this scholarly curiosity as a weakness, because Chet Douglas often got "carried away" and would pursue a topic while the class went on to other subjects. Thus, despite Finny's taunt that he cannot beat out his boy for top academic honors, Gene calculates that he can and grows more and more certain that he will become the best student in the school. As if to hold back the impending calamity to be caused by Gene's hostility toward Finny, the serene forces of nature almost overcome his hatred: "Sometimes I found it hard to remember his treachery, sometimes I discovered myself thoughtlessly slipping back into affection for him again. It was hard to remember when one summer day after another broke with cool effulgence over us, and there was a breath of widening life in the morning air. . . . It was hard to remember in the heady and sensual clarity of these mornings; I forgot whom I hated and who hated me. I wanted to break out crying from stabs of hopeless joy, or intolerable promise, or because these mornings were too full of beauty for me, because I knew of too much hate to be contained in a world like this" (47). Feeling like a pagan, intoxicated by the very oxygen he breathed, Gene is reminiscent of Emily Dickinson's little tippler who reels through endless summer days. While nature seems to hold life in a state of suspended animation, August arrives, a month with portents of conclusions, which arouses "a final fullness everywhere. . . ." The mood of languor and repose here is deceptive, however, and Knowles has created this wonderfully evocative description to provide a moment of hiatus prior to bringing down the curtain on the first act of his drama, which closes as it began—at the tree.

Finny entices Gene to leave off his studies once again and to accompany him to the river to watch Leper Lepellier jump from the tree and qualify for the Suicide Society. Gene is suspicious that Finny has put the whole thing up to ruin his grade on the French examination. Finny, however, is truly astonished to learn that Gene prefers to study rather than goof off. Furthermore, he reveals that he did not think Gene needed to study—that his grades came as naturally as sports came to Finny. This revelation is a shock to Finny, but Gene's conclusions are even more shocking. He comes to understand that there had never been any rivalry between them, at least not on Finny's part. He is wrong in his original assumption, and this is confirmed by Finny's sincere urging that he resume his studies rather than come with them to the tree. The sudden awareness that Finny never envied him, had never been motivated by duplicity or treachery, shrivels Gene's self-concept; he is overwhelmed by his own smallness: "Any fear I had ever had of the tree was nothing beside this. It wasn't my neck, but my understanding which was menaced. He had never been jealous of me for a second. Now I knew that there never was and never could have been any rivalry between us. I was not of the same quality as he. I couldn't stand this" (51). Gene's conception of his worth has been totally reversed. Only a short time before he had felt that Finny was "no better than I was, no matter who won all the contests" (48). Now that Gene's diagnosis of Finny's case is revealed as mistaken, he is reduced to a state of listless humiliation, shocked to the core of his being because his intelligence was inadequate and his conception of Finny all false. Against Finny's insistence that he remain at his books, he leaves his studying to follow the group of boys going to Leper's initiation into the Suicide Society. As the procession moves toward the river, their "gigantic shadows" are ominously cast across the campus while Gene's mind is "exploring the new dimensions of isolation," suggesting the trauma he is experiencing.

Once the tree is reached, the crucial scene unfolds. Finny, in an elevated mood, delighted by the occasion and the fading glow of the day, suggests to Gene a double jump, side by side, perhaps as an emblematic gesture of the new understanding between them. Gene, however, feels no sense of exuberance, only numbness of spirit as he follows Finny up the tree. On the limb their positions are reversed from the earlier double jump—Finny is now farthest out on the limb and in the most dangerous position. It will be recalled that when Gene was in this situation and he momentarily lost his balance, Finny had saved him from falling by instinctively reaching out a hand to him. But now, as Finny balances on the branch, Gene—in an inexplicable act of vindictiveness that in moral ambiguity is perhaps only rivaled by the killing of the albatross by the ancient mariner, or by Mersault's murder of the Arab in *The Stranger*—bends his knees and shakes the limb, making Finny lose his balance and fall to the bank below with a "sickening and unnatural thud."

This act of betrayal is obviously unpremeditated; Gene has not indicated to the reader that he planned to do any harm to his friend. Indeed, the reader is prepared for just the opposite. Tragically, though, Gene does not yet understand himself. While he feels humbled by Finny's goodness, he can't stand it that he is inferior, so in an impulsive act—a "reflex," as Knowles once called it to an audience at the Air Force Academy—Gene jars his friend out of the tree to bring him down to a level where he can compete with him again. Although there is no reason to believe that Gene desired to murder or maim Finny, he clearly wants to embarrass him, to cut him down to size. Significantly,

"The tree was tremendous, an irate, steely black steeple
beside the river."
Photograph courtesy of Phillips Exeter Academy.

this fall that Gene causes results in "the first clumsy physical action I
had ever seen him make" (52). The immediate effect of Gene's action
is a sense of catharsis. For the moment Gene is liberated from the
tension of his rivalry, and in "unthinking surrender," he jumps from
the tree without fear for what he has done or is doing.

This is the most disturbing event thus far in the narrative, and for the first time the reader comprehends why the narrator has returned to the tree after fifteen years. In terms of the dramatic structure it is clearly the defining event. Everything has pointed to this major complication, and all that follows in the novel will revolve around it. In the subsequent chapters Gene and Finny struggle to come to terms with what happened in the tree, and it is an episode that deserves more extensive analysis in order to be comprehended fully.

In the essay entitled "The Young Writer's Real Friends," Knowles suggests that writers should not explain or tell their readers too much. He asks, "Why go through the exhausting labor of creating characters and a place and a time and so on if you are going to destroy their effect by telling the reader much about them?" The point of the argument is that readers should work out their own understanding of what a work of literature means to them in light of their own education and experience, and it is with this advice in mind that we should reflect what has transpired up through the first fifty pages in the fictional world that Knowles has given us. In the same essay cited above, Knowles has said that in writing *A Separate Peace* he eschewed artificial complexities и id left symbolism alone. However, much as he may have avoided these literary effects, he did wind up with a novel that has several levels of meaning, that has a symbolic pattern, that contains metaphysical paradoxes, and that features an underlying myth.

The episode at the tree is nothing less than a representation of the loss of innocence and the acquisition of knowledge—a knowledge of evil and eventually, a knowledge of self. Finny's fall from the tree divides the novel thematically, and Gene's jump immediately afterward is a ritual of passage for him, marking a permanent change in his understanding of himself and the world that comes with the transition from innocence to experience—a move from the warm, Eden-like summer world to the realities of the coming winter term, during which Gene must come to terms with his sin and try to reestablish contact with the grace he lost by his deceit at the tree.

Which returns us to the question, why did Gene do it? Many commentators have offered their explanations of Gene's motives. Some find the cause in Gene's envy—he simply can't allow Finny to be his superior in every way. Others argue that the cause is more complex psychologically, that Gene and Finny's relationship is a variation of the *Doppelgänger* motif and that Gene has to destroy his alter ego in order to win back his identity. Finny's character is a projection of a part of Gene's personality that he wants to destroy, the primitive, lawless, and archaic side that threatens his process of socialization and adult maturation.

In stories with the theme of the Double or *Doppelgänger,* the central character confronts another person who represents the other self. The concept of the Double is largely the result of the analysis of folk superstitions and beliefs vis-à-vis modern literature. A study by Otto Rank showed that the belief in doubles is a phenomenon that has existed in primitive cultures and has evolved down through the centuries, receiving special attention in the twentieth century because of Freud's theories about the large role played by irrationality in human behavior. Modern psychological studies have theorized that each of us has within us a shadow self, a Double who is a manifestation of the antisocial tendencies of the id. The reasons for the origins of these beliefs in the west are complex and go back to the Middle Ages and the rise of Christianity, with its belief in a dual human nature of body and soul, one good and the other evil. Intellectual movements like romanticism in the nineteenth century that focused on the inner being and the outer personality of man also created a conscious preoccupation with human nature in terms of opposing selves. This was especially true in literature where there was greater emphasis than ever on introspection, the irrational, and the fantastic. *A Separate Peace,* with its center of concern being characterization, exploited the Double motif more than other genres, much like Stevenson's *Dr. Jekyll and Mr. Hyde,* Dostoyevski's *The Double,* Melville's *Pierre,* Emily Brontë's *Wuthering Heights* and Conrad's *The Secret Sharer,* to name a few.

The appeal of the double motif to novelists was that it was a means by which the mental struggles of the characters in a work of fiction could be revealed in terms that were plausible. Modern readers expected realism in novels, and the allegorical representations of alternate states of being used in the *psychomachias* or struggle for the soul in medieval morality plays could no longer serve the purpose. Modern psychology has further refined the concept of the Double, making the two components of character representative of the rational and instinctive side of human nature; the clash between the conscious and the unconscious life and the reconciliation between the dual sides of personality become the equivalents of tragic and fortunate outcomes. The disintegration and loss of personality are the ultimate tragedy in terms of mental disorders, while coming to terms with the conflicting selves (the shadow and the anima in Jungian terms) leads to adjustment and acceptance that is the ultimate fortunate outcome—a psychic comedy in short.

As Claire Rosenfield has pointed out in her article "The Shadow Within," the twentieth century novelists make conscious use of and exploit the theories of the Double.[27] She peaces *A Separate Peace* within the tradition of the *Doppelgänger* novel because of the way Knowles applies the double motif to teenage characters who are coping with the issue of identity and self-discovery even more intensely than adults characters would. In her analysis of the way the Double pattern applies to *A Separate Peace*, she describes Finny as the principle of anarchy, a rule-breaker who reacts intuitively rather than logically to situations. Gene, on the other hand, is inhibited and repressed by rules. Finny lives in a child's spontaneous world, while Gene is on the threshold of adulthood and is much more concerned with his self-image and his status than his friend. It is obvious from what we have seen of the two boys that they both complement and contradict each other. Gene is a scholar and Finny an athlete; one is conventional and the other unconventional, but they are also similar in many ways. For example, they are the same age, with birthdays in the fall; they are also about the same size and strength. Thus, they are bodily doubles but psychologially estranged. Gene's instinctive attraction to Finny and his inability to resist his hypnotic influence are due to his attraction to the primitive energy that Finny manifests, a pull Gene is trying to resist. His anxiety and tension during their relationship in the summer session of 1942 can be traced to alternating feelings of attraction and repulsion toward Finny. Therefore, when Gene commits the irrational act that cripples Finny, he is on an unconscious level striking out at that side of himself that he has projected into Finny and that he can make disappear by shaking him loose from the tree and dropping him out of sight.[28] Indeed, when Finny falls, it is as if he has been magically banished, and Gene leaps into the river with a sense that he is free of all apprehension. Having purged himself of his Double whom he thinks he can never compete with on equal terms, he seeks to cleanse himself symbolically of his second self in the river's water.

Rosenfield's interpretation of the conflict along the lines of the Doppelganger theme touches on a main issue of the novel, but it raises some questions and avoids others. She, for instance, does not take into account that Gene's hostility toward Finny at the critical moment is a result of his sense that Finny is superior to him, and that it is this particular realization that Gene cannot abide. Phineas is not riddled with envy; he has no enmity toward Gene; Gene is totally outclassed and an abject failure before Finny. Furthermore, after the accident Gene attempts to appropriate Finny's qualities rather than reject "the irrational externalized by Finny." In fact, Gene's final realization about Finny is that he was his friend rather than his enemy. Therefore, the greater irony of the aggression against Finny is that if Gene is attempting on some subliminal level to eliminate what Finny represents within himself, he is killing the better half of his own personality, which was Finny's innocence, his essential purity.

Although it is Finny who has fallen physically, the more significant fall here is Gene's, which has moral and psychological dimensions. It is apparent that Knowles's intention is that these events, which take place at this tree during an idyllic summer—the last time the boys enjoy the freedoms of peace before they have to prepare for war—should parallel the biblical fall from grace that occurs by a forbidden tree in the Garden of Eden. There are, however, some notable differences between the two situations that do not permit the novel to be taken as a simple allegory of the loss of paradise and the commission of original sin. For one thing, as Paul Witherington has pointed out, Knowles creates a much more ambiguous conflict in his treatment of character and symbol at this critical juncture in the history.[29] While the parallels between Eden and Devon in the summer of 1942 seem pat enough, Devon is an insular sort of paradise, a pastoral world of academe within a historical world that has already fallen very far indeed into the evils of a global conflict. So, while the boys read Virgil and play their games, bombs are falling on central Europe. It is a world of innocence that must inevitably be broken, and the boys cannot escape being tested by the hard facts of reality.

The immersion into that harsh reality and the revelations of our limitations as human beings are what Knowles attempts to symbolize by the fall from the tree. There is no physical or metaphysical serpent as such that coils about its trunk, but it is still as much the tree of knowledge, and its fruit is bitter. There is a snake that menaces and tempts the momentary peace the boys live, but it is a bosom serpent—as Hawthorne calls the latent evil in the human heart. It is this unfelt or unconscious hostility that we all have programmed into us that causes Gene to bend his knees and spring the limb "like a piston," bringing down Finny as a result of some kind of reflex action, which can only be called original sin for the lack of a better term. There are parallels between what happens to Gene and what happens in Genesis, but the echoes are surely ironic. Finny, who actually falls in body, is totally unaware of evil until his second fall. Gene, on the other hand, falls spiritually but not physically. However, his awareness of evil makes him a greater sufferer than Finny, who almost until the very end of the novel suffers only physically, rather than spiritually.[30]

Leslie Fiedler, in a 1958 essay entitled "The Eye of Innocence," offers an insightful analysis of the initiation motif in American literature, which can be applied to *A Separate Peace* with great profit, although Fiedler is never directly concerned with Knowles's novel. (*A Separate Peace* had not at that point been published.) According to Fiedler, "an initiation is a fall through knowledge to maturity; behind it there persists the myth of the Garden of Eden, the assumption that to know good and evil is to be done with joy of innocence and to take on the burdens of work and childbearing and death."[31] Fiedler argues that a concern with an initiation in evil explains the shift in fiction to a concern with adolescence, and Huckleberry Finn is the prototype of the innocent on the verge of experience. The most interesting aspect of Fiedler's thesis for an understanding of *A Separate Peace* as an initiation story is his belief that in American literature it is through violence rather than sex and through death rather than love that the adolescent enters the fallen world.[32]

Fielder says the transition from child to man is not worked out in the overt sexual terms of continental literature, and he finds that the reason is a "genteel reticence" on the part of American authors, reared in the puritan tradition. There is, nevertheless, a covert handling of sexual initiation in American literature. Since Knowles was writing in the repressed 1950s rather than the liberated 1980s, he represses any sexually overt overtones in the intense friendship between Gene and Finny. One French commentator, George-Michael Sarotte, has not been so reticent about pointing out the homosexual implications in his book, *Like a Brother, Like a Lover*. He discusses the relationship between the two boys in light of what is identified as one of the "four archetypes of the homosexual couple."[33] In this particular relationship, which flourishes in the all-male universe of a boys' school, "friendship changes into hatred out of fear of its changing into love" (45). Gene resents Finny's physical dominance of him, which creates an anxiety of becoming "a passive element in their union," and, according to Sarotte, he fears that in "attaching himself to Finny he would come to love him; [thus] Gene's hatred of Finny reveals his refusal to eroticize the desire for identification with him." So, by this line of reasoning, Gene's act in the tree is an attempt to emasculate Finny and to destroy an ideal that he cannot conform to. In doing so, Gene causes himself much sexual maladjustment and frustration for having "mislaid his own identity" and yoked himself for the next fifteen years of his life to a "powerful neurosis." In Sarotte's interpretation of the events that primarily cause the catastrophe, the fault lies with Gene's suppression of his homoerotic attraction for Finny. Whether the deep affection the two boys feel for each other has any physical basis, it is difficult to say. Gene is obviously very observant about Finny's appearance, size, features, and dress, but this preoccupation with the bodily Phineas is in part demanded by Gene's role as narrator—he must create an image of this character for the reader.

Knowles himself pointed out in a 1972 interview in *Ingenue* that "Finny and Gene were in love—not physically but emotionally—the book shows that there is nothing wrong with that."[34] Because of the first-person narrative method we cannot know Finny's thoughts or feelings about Gene, but we assume that they are much less complex and ambiguous than Gene's, who is clearly both attracted and repelled by Finny. Whatever it is that exactly triggers his aggression is anyone's guess. His hostility and destructiveness can be laid down to several causes: to original sin; to something ignorant in the human; to fear of his Double, his negative psychological counterpart; or to latent homosexual feelings, which cause him, as Oscar Wilde says, to try to kill the thing he loved.

To ascribe any one motive to explain Gene's action would be reductive; it is the result of a "darker streak in human nature" that can be explained theologically, psychologically, and sociologically.

CHAPTER 7

After the Fall

In the aftermath of the "accident," Gene waits with great apprehension, since he fully expects to be held responsible for Finny's fall. After several days go by and he is not called in to make an account, he realizes Finny is not going to report him and that he need not fear an accusation by his friend. He decides that Finny is waiting to have an open confrontation with him rather than to accuse him behind his back. Gene's reading of Finny's motives, however, leads again to a false conclusion; he has once more projected his thinking onto Finny. In fact, Finny is never able to bring himself to accuse Gene.

Finny's accident is hard not only on Gene but on the Devon teaching staff as well. Gene notes that they seemed to feel as if it were a great injustice that a sixteen-year-old should have been struck down during the last free and happy summer before facing preparations for war. To make Gene's guilt even more acute, everyone discusses the incident with him endlessly on the assumption that he wants to talk about it, being the closest eyewitness and Finny's roommate. Gene's heavy burden of guilt is almost too much for him to bear. Seeking solitude, he retreats to his room; there he attempts to make his mind a blank, to forget who, where, and what he is. In this frame of mind, an idea occurs to Gene that shakes him out of the apathy of guilt for the moment. He decides to put on Finny's clothes—a rather obvious effort to efface his own identity and assume Finny's. In this highly ironic scene, Gene, alone in his room, dons Finny's pink shirt, trousers, and shoes, covertly accepting his resemblance to and kinship with Finny, a relationship that he has not being willing to acknowledge until this point. Finny's attitude toward wearing Gene's clothes was just the opposite—he wore them as if they were his own. Gene, always conscious of ownership, would never have picked up the nearest garment at hand and worn it, but Finny was indifferent because, as Gene comes to realize, "Phineas had thought of me as an extension of himself." By attiring himself in Finny's clothes, Gene takes the first step in what will be a profound experience of self-evaluation. Through a series of acts of identification with Finny, he will keep alive the very side of himself that he had earlier sought to suppress. Eventually, he will come to see himself as Finny, but at this terrible moment he wants to hide from himself as much as acquire a new persona.

There is something introspective and neurotic about what Gene does that is tantamount to an identity crisis. Putting on Finny's clothing makes Gene feel, uncannily, as if Finny had been a part of him all along. In this moment of harmony, the opposed modes of Gene's being—the intuitive and atavistic symbolized by Finny and rational and civilized represented in himself—are for once reconciled, and he feels ennobled. After sliding into Finny's luxurious pink shirt, he says, "the rich material against my skin excited a sense of strangeness and distinction; I felt like some nobleman, some Spanish grandee" (54). Yet the transformation that counts most fully is the one that occurs when he looks in the mirror; he is "no remote aristocrat . . . no character out of daydreams. I was Phineas, Phineas to the life. I even had his humorous expression in my face, his sharp, optimistic awareness. I had no idea why this gave me such intense relief, but it seemed, standing there in Finny's triumphant shirt, that I would never stumble through the confusions of my own character again" (54).

For as long as the illusion lasts, Gene is at peace. He sleeps well that night, but upon waking up he is brought back to the reality of his

own guilty personality and of what he has done. The remainder of
chapter is devoted to Gene's two unsuccessful attempts to confess
crime to Finny. After learning from the kindly infirmary doctor t
Finny's injury is worse than he feared and that "sports will be out"
him, he is stricken. Ironically, the doctor urges Gene to help Fi
come to terms with this fact. Shackled with this awful responsibi
and filled with trepidation, he goes to the hospital. Finny, however,
mind still clouded by drugs and doubts, does not accuse Gene, adı
ting only to a "feeling." Gene's fear and suspicion of Finny are
evident during this interview. Gene's first question to Finny is a pr
to discover how much he knows: "What happened at the tree?
How did you fall, how could you fall off like that?" (57) In a statem
full of dramatic irony, he accuses Finny of trying to drag him dowr
reaching out for his hand. Finny replies that he only wanted to g
hold of his hand so that he wouldn't fall off the limb. There
moment when Finny comes close to realizing the truth. He recalls
odd expression on Gene's face and says, "But I don't see why
should look so personally shocked. You look like it happened to
or something"—to which Gene says, with more truth than he reali
"It's almost like it did! I was right there, right on the limb beside y
(57). At this point it appears as if Finny will accuse Gene, but he
only a hunch rather than a hard conviction and is unwilling to p
Gene simply because he feels something is wrong. This is somethin
a role reversal for Finny, who normally would not hesitate from sta
his opinion. However, it is Finny's intuitive understanding that the
truth would be too shameful for either of them to confront, and
backs off, saying, "It was a crazy idea . . . I just fell, that's all." Finı
apology for harboring a suspicion so base rebukes Gene, who po:
lates a "Finnyesque" commandment regarding the ethics of persc
contact: "Never accuse a friend of a crime if you only have a feeling
did it" (58). Of course, the corollary to this commandment applies
Gene, but he cannot come to terms with it: "Never commit a cr
against your friend." Shamed by Finny's compassion for him and
realization that Finny would tell the truth if the rules were revers
Gene attempts to make a clean breast of his part in the accide

However, the doctor's untimely return prevents it, and Gene does not have another opportunity to confess until after summer school closes.

Returning to school in September from vacation at his home in Georgia, Gene makes a second attempt to tell Finny the full story. Driven by a compulsive urge, he takes a taxi to a Boston suburb to Finny's home instead of catching the next train to New Hampshire. It is important to note that Gene's trip to make a full confession to Finny is a spontaneous act. He does not premeditate it; it is a natural act of contrition. He instinctively tells the cabdriver to go to Finny's address rather than the train station, his voice giving the directions as though someone else were speaking.

Gene is astonished to see the alteration in his friend. No longer the healthy athlete, Finny is in a weelchair and looks like the invalid Gene has feared he might become. In response to a question about what happened to him down south, Gene relates the story of a brush fire that got out of control and threatened his family's house, finally requiring the fire department to put it out. The story is a stall and a way of passing time during an awkward moment, but here, as is so often the case in this novel, even the least relevant details convey some thematic significance, and the fires that Gene describes burning on his parents' place are not as hot as the burning guilt that sears his conscience. But he does not know how to broach the subject of what happened at the tree after the small talk about his vacation. Gene is further put off by the strange surroundings and feels like an intruder in this house. The domestic context is much different from the dormitory situation where he had previously known Finny, and he is somewhat disoriented psychologically. Amid the civilized period furniture and family pictures in the room, he has the sensation that he is now more out of touch with his friend than ever. He compares himself to "a wild man who had stumbled in from the jungle to tear the place apart" (61). Paradoxically, while in this frame of mind, Gene is sitting in an early American chair whose rigid back and armrests force him into "a righteous posture." In this upright position Gene opens up the subject of the accident, making his best effort to be candid and forthcoming. Finny refuses to believe him, even after Gene tells him, "I deliberately

jounced the limb so you would fall off" (62). The exchange breaks down into an irrational confrontation; Finny threatens to hit Gene if he does not shut up. Gene, on the other hand, is relieved because he sees that even Finny can have destructive feelings and thus might understand that his behavior in the tree was motivated by a similar impulse. At last, realizing that his attempt to force a confession on Finny will only inflict more pain, Gene decides to defer forcing the issue and to make it up to Finny back at Devon. He retracts his words and makes an awkward exit, promising Finny that he will continue to live outside the rules as they had done during the summer session, but knowing in his heart that he is telling a lie.

One of the consequences of the fall brought out in this chapter is the fear of facing the truth. Both boys have gained a terrible new knowledge but neither can face it. Gene, in the first confession scene, evades the truth, and it is Finny in the second who is evasive. The rest of the novel will be concerned with showing how the sin that was committed at the tree is worked out through forgiveness and an understanding of what caused the evil. As the two confession scenes suggest, a full expiation of the guilt cannot be achieved by a mere confrontation; confession alone is not sufficient for release, and at this point it only causes more mutual pain because neither can do more than deal in half-truths.

In the subsequent scenes of the novel, which show the spiritually crippled Gene attempting to atone to the physically crippled Finny, the atmosphere is far different; there has been a radical change in the weather, in both literal and symbolic terms. The laxity in deportment that had been permitted in the summer is not tolerated in the regular fall term, and rules and routines are now more strictly enforced. Gene realizes that without Finny "peace had deserted Devon," and he longs for the bygone days of summer when things had been made more authenic by Finny's presence. Although it is only September, there is "an edge of coolness," implying the coming of winter, and the dreaming calm of the "gipsy summer" gives way to "a new and energetic wind" that has dropped the first leaves from the trees. To Gene there is an air of imposture about the school. The faculty and their families are held in mild contempt by Gene, who wonders what these husbands and wives could have ever found attractive in each other. One of the young teachers back on leave in his navy officer's uniform looks incongruous with his insipid face rising above his dashing outfit. Ironically, the school policy during this the first term of the war year 1942 to 1943 is "continuity." The emphasis is on upholding the 163-year-old traditions of Devon. From Gene's standpoint these traditions have already been abandoned for "the Duration," the phrase used at the time to indicate the suspension of something until the war was over, such as maid service in the boys' rooms.

The sermon that Gene hears on the opening day of school in the chapel is especially grating to him in his excited state of mind. The boys are exhorted to think about what they owed Devon; he and Finny, in contrast, had thought of themselves first and what the school owed them. Gene's reaction to the voice of officialdom indicates an emerging change in his personality. He is ascribing to a point of view Finny would have endorsed—an attitude that is counter to the establishment view. Perhaps even more to the point is Gene's "chilled" reaction to the service, especially the hymn that italicizes the theme of guilt, "Dear Lord and Father of Mankind, Forgive Our Foolish Ways." The grim reminder in the lines of this puritan hymn of original sin is in marked contrast to the rhythm of the "wayward gipsy music" that the boys had moved to during the summer. It was a music, Gene realizes, that he had nearly learned to respond to, but one that had come to an end in the "last long rays of daylight at the tree, when Phineas fell" (65).

Without Finny's moral support, Gene does not have the courage to question authority. The meaning that he takes from the sermon is that it is fatal to break the rules; echoing one of Hemingway's heroes, Lt. Frederic Henry, Gene concludes, "if you break the rules, then they break you." Thus, Gene decides to keep a low profile and not to tempt fate again. His summer experience has taught him caution, and he is now fully aware of his capacity for antisocial behavior.

Gene's reaction to the intrusion of a new boy, Brinker Hadley—the big man on campus—into the room once occupied by Leper

Lepellier is a further indication of the changes in Gene's character. He realizes that once he would have gravitated toward a person like Brinker, whose status as the "year's dominant student" would, in Gene's eyes, have made him a person to cultivate as a friend, but oddly he now finds that he prefers the vagueness of Leper and misses his trays of snail collections, which have been replaced by Brinker's file cabinets. The experience of the summer, the influence of the gypsy days, has created an affinity with the natural world, symbolized by Leper's snails, the motes of dust in the sunbeams, and the ivy that creeps in at the windows. Brinker's plans for success in the social scheme of the schoolboy world have no appeal for Gene.

A new inability to make schedules and to keep up with time afflicts Gene. The very biorhythms that once governed him have been upset; Gene had once described himself as "a walking clock" and knew exactly what time it was during the escapade to the beach with Finny. Now, he has acquired another trait of Finny's, almost as if he wants to become what Finny was as a means to escape from himself. His most obvious attempt to efface his personality is his decision to take on the most anonymous extracurricular activity he can—assistant crew manager, a position usually held by a lowerclassman or someone with a physical handicap. Since Gene is a senior and has athletic potential, his decision to hold this job is masochistic, to say the least.

The humiliation Gene seeks is found in two episodes in this chapter. The first involves a confrontation with an arrogant classmate whose ugly personality is amplified by his name, Cliff Quackenbush. The trouble between them breaks out because of Quackenbush's open contempt toward Gene for copping out as assistant crew manager. He seems to suspect that Gene is hiding some defect, but Gene knows he is too egocentric and too ignorant to detect what is really troubling him. During an argument, Quackenbush calls Gene "a maimed son-of-a-bitch," which is closer to the truth than he realizes. Ironically, in the fight that subsequently breaks out between them, Gene feels that he is fighting for Finny and for the honor of all who are crippled, but he is also lashing out at something else. He is striking out at ignorance, the sort of blindness he once knew that had prevented him from accepting the gypsy summer on its own terms and that now makes the memory of "skylarks, splashes, and petal-bearing breezes" so hard to endure because they have been lost. He hates Quackenbush also because he is the antithesis of Finny; he is the adult world of punitive authority personified, whose very tone of voice, unlike the music of Finny's hypnotic speech, has "matured" too soon and sounds remote as though spoken through a tube. Gene's contempt for him is heightened because this boy, who he thinks "knows nothing and feels nothing as Phineas had done," has been able to touch at the core of his problem with one of his accusations, saying sarcastically, "Who the hell are you anyway?" It is a remark that causes an "inward groan" in Gene, who realizes that he is in the midst of an identity crisis, that he is maimed in spirit because he crippled his friend in body.

Everywhere in this chapter the unpleasant present is juxtaposed to pleasing memories of the recent past. For example, while on his way to the boathouse located along the saltwater Naguamsett River, which flows below the freshwater Devon River, he is reminded of Finny's exploits on this more appealing water. Gone are his recollections of the tree and the pain he created; instead he sees Phineas "in exaltation, balancing on one foot on the prow of a canoe like a river god, his raised arms invoking the air to support him, face transfigured . . . his skin glowing from immersions, his whole body hanging between river and sky as though he had transcended gravity and might by gently pushing upward with his foot glide a little way higher and remain suspended in space, encompassing all the glory of summer and offering it to the sky" (67).

In contrast to this epiphany of Finny remembered in a moment of apotheosis is the evil troll of the ugly, salty river, Quackenbush, the presiding genius of this other shore. Unlike Finny, he is not of the water like a demigod but rather a factotum, who serves as a "crew manager." In the images employed here, the two rivers are also significant for defining the dual existence that Gene has experienced. The lower river, the Naguamsett, is a tidal river. Its banks are fringed with ugly mud and seaweed and the water is saline. As Knowles describes it, this river's movements were "governed by unimaginable factors like the

Gulf Stream, the Polar Ice Cap, and the moon," whereas the freshwater Devon, which headed above, followed a course "determined by some familiar hills a little inland; it rose among highland farms and forests which we knew . . ." (68). In Gene's mind the river's flow takes on symbolic meaning. The saltwater river with its primitive Indian name is dark and doubtful, its life controlled by alien forces, while the Devon with its British name is redolent of the tranquility of domesticated waters, much like those that Constable painted flowing through his serene landscapes. It comes from known and familiar country. It should be noted as well that, in a deliberate pairing of the symbols, one river is associated with summer and the other with winter. The Devon, with its links to the Edenic time of summer, is counterpointed against the Naguamsett, into whose cold waters Gene falls during his fight at the boat house. The water motif implies an immersion into a harsher reality. It is, however, an ironic reversal of the sacrament of baptism because, instead of purifying Gene, it makes him feel even dirty. The salty, sticky waters of the winter river have to be washed off by a bath, and Gene himself says, "the Naguamsett was something else entirely . . . it seemed appropriate that my *baptism* [emphasis added] there had taken place on the first day of this winter session, and that I had been thrown into it, in the middle of a fight" (78). Gene's reflection helps the reader to evaluate the meaning of this episode, which shows Gene paying homage to Finny's spirit by trying to understand the world as Finny did; his mind is already becoming "Phineas filled," and he has begun the restorative process that began with his identification with Finny when he put on the pink shirt and will evolve eventually into his acquiring a sense of his own self.

The last humiliation that befalls Gene on his first day back at school for the winter term is his encounter with one of the regular Devon masters, Mr. Ludsbury, who dresses him down for being out of line at the moment and for "slipping in any number of ways since last year." This subtle rebuke carries with it a great deal of dramatic irony, for both the reader and Gene read far more into the word "slipped" than the master does. It is understated indeed from Gene's point of view, who feels he has played the part of Judas to his friend. That summer, which Mr. Ludsbury says was a time when "everything went straight to seed," is a period that Gene now regards as his lost Eden, where Phineas had presided over the "gaming" that so disturbed the moral rectitude of authority figures like Mr. Ludsbury. Gene upbraids himself bitterly, thinking, "If only I had . . . seized and held and prized the multitudes of advantages the summer offered me; if only I had" (74).

A final reprimand comes from Finny in the form of an unexpected long distance call. Concerned about Gene's behavior while he had been in Boston, Finny calls to wish him a happy return to school and to satisfy himself that Gene is not having a nervous breakdown. He also wants to make sure that Gene is willing to keep him as a room-mate when he returns to school. Reassured on these points, Finny is aghast that Gene is not going out for a sport and chides him roundly for taking such a humble job as assistant crew manager. Again Gene cannot honestly tell Finny his motives, that since they were prohibited to Finny by Dr. Stanpole, he too has forfeited sports as an act of atonement. Finny cuts through Gene's weak protest that he is too busy for athletics with a strong imperative: "Listen, pal, if *I* can't play sports, *you're* going to play them for me" (77), a request Gene cannot refuse. In fact, it provides Gene with a sense of purpose that he has not had since the fall. He commits himself without reserve to Finny and realizes "with a soaring sense of freedom revealed that this must have been my purpose from the first: to become a part of Phineas" (77).

Although Gene will be rejuvenated by Finny's return, there is an intervening bleak period for him. He undergoes another mortifying experience, this time at the hands of Brinker Hadley, when Gene is put through a mock trial in the Butt Room, where the boys go to smoke. In a scene that is ripe with dramatic irony and full of portent, Gene is taken down to the smoking area—jokingly called the "dungeon"—in order to get at the truth about what Gene did to Finny. It is all in fun from Brinker's point of view; he is merely following up a droll charge that Gene "fixed it" so he could have a room to himself, but the humor hurts Gene, who is accused of the "rankest treachery" and told that what he did was "practically fratricide." In a remark that foreshadows events to come, Brinker promises Gene that he will have his day in court. He is accused of lying and trying "to weasel out of it with a false confession" (81). The jest goes too far for Gene when the scene of the crime is identified as the tree by the river. Gene tries to go along with the charade, but he is unable to confess again, even in a joking way. As he is reconstructing the crime, he gags when he attempts to say that he pushed Finny out of the tree. Fortunately for Gene, he is able to extricate himself with a bit of sarcasm and to escape from the riding of his inquisitors, who had little idea of how close they were to the truth. Gene is shaken by this inquisition, even though it was in jest, and he is not by any means sure that he has laid their suspicions to rest, having given them a clue of his real guilt by being too nervous to smoke.

The reader can hardly fail to see that in the scenes in the Butt Room and at the boat house, Gene has been laid upon by accusers who do not fully comprehend how their jibes exacerbate his feelings of guilt. Quackenbush and Brinker have each inadvertently rubbed salt in his wounds. The former taunts him with the word "maimed," which, of course, describes Gene's psychological condition, and the latter calls Gene a "prisoner," which indeed he is, held captive by fear and guilt for a deed that he has neither truly confessed to nor yet atoned for. The inquiry into Gene's guilt is put aside for the moment in Chapter 7, and Knowles returns to the theme of the war again. In mid-October the Devon boys twice offer their services to the war effort as volunteers, first to help harvest the local apple crop and again to shovel snow off the railroad tracks along the main line. A subtle irony is apparent in the apple orchard harvesting, which is more like an outing for the students because they are excused from classes and at the same time paid for their labor. Although they are involved in the job only because of the war, it is still remote, and harvesting apples is too bucolic a task to be anything more than boring. There is a suggestion that the "shining days" the boys spend gathering the apples are a last reprise of Eden, and in what seems a tongue-in-cheek parody of Keats's "Ode to Autumn," Knowles offers an "Apple Ode," composed for the occasion by the sardonic Brinker, who belittles his classmates' contribution to the war effort with these terse lines: "Our chore / is the core / of the war." Knowles contrasts the changing climate and the outlook on the war through an evocative description of the season's first snowfall. It is a snow that is conveyed through military imagery—the big flakes gathering "like noiseless invaders conquering because they took possession so gently" (84). This first snow is followed by another, harder snowfall that stays. Gene draws the parallel between the weather and the war: "In the same way the war, beginning almost humorously with announcements about maids and days spent at apple-picking, commenced its invasion of the school. The early snow was commandeered as its advance guard" (84).

The snow is taken as a premonition of harder times to come, and Gene, who has been initiated into the world of experience, anticipates the changes that the war will soon make in the lives of his generation. His forboding is contrasted to the naive Leper Lepellier, always unaware and unprepared—the person, Gene says, "who was most often and most emphatically taken by surprise, by this and every other shift in our life at Devon." On the day that Gene and two hundred classmates volunteer to shovel snow off the main railroad tracks, everyone except Leper signs up. Instead, Gene encounters him on a pair of antique touring skis, on his way to take pictures of beaver dams on a stream below the school, in an effort to understand better how the "beavers adapt to the winter." This remark in itself is not important, but in the developing context of events it is, like so many details of scene and dialogue in this novel, a portent. Leper himself will be a victim of the changed climate of war and peace; he, ironically, will not be able to adapt to the coming winter as well as the beavers.

Inserted into the casual conversation between Gene and Leper is another ominous remark about overland skiing. Gene is skeptical about this odd sport and urges Leper to find a steep hill to get a fast run down, to which Leper objects, saying that skis should be put to useful purposes, not for foolish racing. Turning his eyes accusingly on Gene, he adds, "You can break a leg with that downhill stuff." Such an approach is all wrong to Leper, not only because it is dangerous, but because the speed prevents one from really looking at the trees passing by. To Leper, the contemplative naturalist, close observation of the nonhuman world is the source of his enjoyment. It is also his way of escaping the mire of human complexities and a way to evade unpleasant realities like war and violence.

After his encounter with Leper, Gene spends the rest of the day in the railroad yards, toiling with shovels to clear the snow off the tracks. In contrast to the larking in the apple orchard, the boys work in gangs under the supervision of a grim old railroad man who dislikes the privileged prep school boys for their wisecracks and youth. A senior version of Quackenbush, the old man spits, grumbles, and orders the boys around throughout the afternoon. When the line is clear and the first train has passed, full of troops—all youthful themselves—the students and soldiers yell back and forth at each other in cheerful greeting. The effect of seeing a whole trainful of young men, not much older than themselves, going off to the greatest adventure of their lives, creates a feeling of envy in the students. The soldiers in their uniforms seem an elite group compared to the Devon boys in their grimy work clothes, and they feel abashed and suddenly juvenile.

The sight of the troop train brings the reality of the war home with greater impact than anything heretofore, and the boys' conversation turns toward talk about enlistment in various military programs and the fear that they are going to miss out on the war and not have war stories to tell grandchildren, since the war may end before they finish school. Brinker seems to be the most frustrated from the lack of involvement in the war, and he grows scornful of the study of Latin at such a time. He especially despises people like Quackenbush, who plans to postpone service as long as possible, and Leper, who is more interested in the lives of beavers than in the war effort. Impulsively, he makes a decision to enlist and thus plants the thought in Gene's mind that this is the solution to his own problem: "To enlist. To slam the door impulsively on the past, to shed everything down to my last bit of clothing, to break the pattern of my life—that complex design I had been weaving since birth with all its dark threads . . . all those tangled threads which required the dexterity of a virtuoso to keep flowing—I yearned to take giant military shears to it, snap! bitten off in an instant, and nothing left in my hands but spools of khaki which would

weave only a plain, flat, khaki design, however twisted they might be"
(92).

Not only would entering the service put Gene's life in the hands of
a simpler fate, it would allow him to channel his latent savagery toward the destruction of war. In the military, his capacity for evil would
have a proper outlet. "The war would be deadly all right. But I was
used to finding something deadly in things that attracted me; there was
always something deadly lurking in anything I wanted, anything I
loved. And if it wasn't there, as for example with Phineas, then I put it
there myself" (92).

Here Gene is on the verge of an irrational decision. The cold
winter stars, casting chilled points of light, are symbolic of the frigid
state of mind Gene is in at this moment. Like the high star that shines
above the men in Stephen Crane's "The Open Boat," these heavens
likewise offer no comfort. The stars evoke in Gene no thoughts of God
or dreams of high romance. With no family, friends, or familiar sky to
guide him, Gene has lost his moorings and gives way to the temptation
to run away and seek another destiny as a soldier. The light imagery
comes in again in a contrapuntal play of symbolism in the last scene of
this chapter. Back in his dorm Gene notices a "warm yellow slab of
light" streaming from under his door. The vitality and brightness of
the light are in sharp contrast to the frigidity of the starlight; they
symbolically herald the return of Phineas, whom Gene finds in the
room at his desk, back just in time to save Gene from submitting his
fate to the military and letting the war take care of everything. Finny
will show Gene the light and keep him on the right path, insuring that
he will come to terms with his evolving identity. Henceforth, he will be
guided by Finny rather than Brinker and will eventually repudiate
those negative forces that war and violence appeal to. Gene had been
on the point of falling, and again he is saved by Finny, who reaches out
and draws him back to himself. With the return of Finny, the "war
passed away" and "peace comes back to Devon" in the mind and
heart of Gene. As if he had intuited Gene's crisis of conscience, Finny
tells him, "I can see I never should have left you alone." When he sees
Finny's pain upon learning his intentions, Gene gives up all plans of

leaving school. Unwilling to hurt Finny again and perhaps realizing that he can find his true integrity by helping the person he has nearly destroyed, Gene determines to stay at Devon and work out his destiny. Once again under Finny's influence, Gene will discover his proper moral purpose and begin his regeneration, a process underscored by the resumption of bedtime prayers by the two boys (but which, according to Finny's dicta, did not last more than three minutes).

The war becomes a distant and unreal thing because of Finny, and once more the boys' focus is on sports instead of combat. Even in the midst of winter, the recommitment to athletics reminds them of the summer's peace. Finny's oddball theory that the war is a hoax even takes over Gene's thinking, and he willingly suspends his disbelief, as much to humor Finny as to beguile himself. According to Finny, the war is just a rumor started by fat old men whose motive is to enslave the spirit of youth, as they had done with Prohibition and the Depression, and to curtail the pleasures of life. The rejection of the war as a fact is, of course, a comic fantasy. Finny himself does not believe in his theory, but he is taking the Blakean stance that a firm persuasion of a thing will make it so, providing an illusion by which both boys can live for a short time longer in an imagined unfallen world of peace.

In this episode the wave of war that had been about to engulf Gene prematurely is turned aside. Finny's timely arrival back at school makes it clear to Gene that he cannot escape the cross he must bear. As surely as Hester and Dimmesdale in *The Scarlet Letter* must remain in New England rather than go back to England to evade the consequences of their sin, so too must Gene work out his guilt at the place where it was incurred. Out of a sense of compunction and gratitude, Gene realizes that he has been saved for the moment: "So the war swept over [me] like a wave at the seashore, gathering power and size as it bore on us, overwhelming in its rush, seemingly inescapable, and then at the last moment eluded by a word from Phineas . . . leaving me peaceably treading water as before. I did not stop to think that one wave is inevitably followed by another even larger and more powerful, when the tide is coming in" (101). Gene's premonition is right, but for this brief period the fancies of Finny will hold sway. He will be under the hypnotic power of Finny's imagination during the whole bleak winter of 1943.

Significantly, on Finny's first day back he decides to cut classes. This time Gene demurs with more vigor before agreeing to go along, showing that he is becoming an equal partner in their relationship. Finny nevertheless prevails upon Gene to go with him to the gym—the place that holds the most meaning for Finny, the site on campus of his triumphs, where the trophy case is full of memorial plaques and cups with his name. It is indicative of Finny's character that many of his awards were for sportsmanship as well as for excellence in the sport; it is even more meaningful that he has gone back to the gym like a pilgrim to a shrine, to seek to restore himself rather than to remember past glories, as Gene had imagined was his motive. As we see, Finny's real motive in bringing Gene to the gym was to pass on the torch. Finny's grasp on reality is such that he knows that his goal to be an Olympic athlete is finished, even though he hides his awareness behind a semiserious joke, confessing that he won't be one hundred percent in shape by 1944. He tells Gene that he is going to have to be "the big star" now that Finny is on the sidelines. Finny's plan is to live vicariously through Gene's athletic exploits. For this transference of power to take place, though, Gene not only has to perform like Finny, but must start to think like Finny. The first lesson to learn is that war is not real but that sports are. Wars are for old men, for adults, while games are for boys, and Finny's instruction is aimed at keeping them boys long enough to accomplish his goal of returning the spirit of peace to the campus. Finny can't change the season or alter what is going on in the outside world, but, as he says of the present time, "the winter loves me . . . I mean as much as you can say a season can love. What I mean is, I love winter, and when you really love something, then it loves you back, in whatever way it has to love" (103). For Gene this sort of benevolent and reciprocal affection is not borne out by the reality of his experience, but he knows that ideally it should be true. The new basis of his friendship with Finny will ultimately depend on this precept. In an act that seems to be one of affirmation and that ironically echoes the archetypal betrayal by Judas, Gene pledges his loyalty to

Finny's dream by doing thirty chin-ups on the parallel bars. Under the influence of Finny's miracle-working voice, he is hypnotized into exceeding himself twice over; having never done more than ten pull-ups, he now does twenty beyond his limit, as Finny counts them off with an urgency that was like "an invisible boost lifting me the distance of my arms, until he sang out 'thirty!' with a flare of pleasure" (109). After this experience and Finny's revelations of his suffering, Gene is convinced that Finny has earned the right to his fantasies and becomes Finny's protégé in mind and body. Now, ironically, it requires an act of imagination on his part to believe in the war, since it is only felt at Devon two-dimensionally through newspapers and photographs. Under Finny's influence, Gene doubts the reality of wartime shortages of meat and gas and the American invasion of Guadacanal.

Gene makes amazing progress under Finny's training program, which teaches Gene how to run through his fatigue and get a second wind. This discovery takes place just before the Christmas holidays and occurs under "a patriarchal elm tree." It is not the tree by the river, however, but one near the headmaster's home, where Finny has laid out a course for Gene to run. In one of the fine descriptive passages that so often punctuate the action of *A Separate Peace,* Knowles writes that "the northern sunshine seemed to pick up faint particles of whiteness floating in the air and powdering the sleek blue sky. Nothing stirred. The bare arching branches of the elm seemed laid into this motionless sky" (111). In the cold blue light of dawn, Gene achieves an almost mystic sense of communion with himself as he again is encouraged by Finny to go beyond his self-imposed limitations. Although there is a "profound seat of pain" in his side, and his knees seem boneless, Gene suddenly feels magnificent, which, Finny explains, is because he found his rhythm; he adds a telling remark that is the key to Gene's dilemma: "You didn't even know anything about yourself" (112). So we see that Finny's return inaugurates a major stage of Gene's regeneration. Instead of the one-sided situation of the summer where Gene suspected Finny of being his rival, the reader finds a growing spirit of collaboration. Gene receives inspiration from Finny on the athletic field and in turn helps Finny by tutoring him in his school work. Both discover how to learn from each other, because, as Gene says, "so much of learning anything depends on the atmosphere in which it is taught" (111).

Again, as is so often the case in this novel, there is a replication of scene in this chapter that sets up a thematic counterpoint. The hookey scene here echoes the first escapade to the beach, except that in the earlier scene, Finny had all his physical vitality. In this second class-cutting episode, Finny is the passive one and Gene has to perform physical feats. The allusion to Lazarus risen from the dead, used to describe Finny at the beach, now has an ironic implication. Finny has risen in a sense; he has come back from the dead, but he is more like Christ in his resurrection than Lazarus because he has a vision of peace. In the end his mission is to heal Gene of the wound that he bears internally. While not wanting to insist too strongly that Knowles is working out an exact scriptural allegory here, the thematic concerns of this chapter are clearly Christian and echo biblical events. Gene and Finny are presented as teacher and disciple. Finny is the savior figure, the sacrificial lamb (even wearing a sheep-lined coat), who has suffered on a tree; Gene, the cause of the fall, is symbolically both Adam and Judas. He has caused the loss of paradise and is guilty of an act of betrayal. The second stage of their relationship is set against a post-Edenic world, but though this paradise is beyond recovery, a second chance is given through Finny, who stands as a second Adam. Gene, the original Adam, will be redeemed by the new Adam through vicarious suffering. Finny's function, like Christ's, is to bring a chance of recovery and to reveal a vision of life of heightened potential.

Finny might have brought off his grand illusion, had it not been for Leper's defection. But the dreamy, overly idealistic Lepellier is the first of the class of 1943 to give up the life of the scholar for that of the soldier. Entranced by a recruiting film of ski troops the "white warriors of winter," who glide silently as angels across pure fields of snow, Leper arrives at the turning point of his life. Only Finny questions the validity of Leper's epiphany, suggesting, with what seems a pun on his name, that the troops in the movie are really Finns who are skiing out to shoot down our allies, the Bolsheviks. Here, as elsewhere, Finny tends to disparage overblown patriotism and to reveal a cynical reserve about the meaning of war where loyalties are changed overnight, our former arch enemies becoming our allies. Leper, however, is convinced by the propaganda film that downhill combat skiing represents an evolution in the art of skiing, a modification or mutation of the sport that has occurred to keep the sport from becoming extinct. In Leper's self-absorbed world, there is no contradiction between the concept of Darwin's theory of survival of the fittest and angelic hosts that sweep down spotless mountainsides. Completing the irony of Leper's conversion to a warrior is the fact that it takes place in the "Renaissance Room;" his "rebirth" will have catastrophic results for him. He leaves for war in one of the most uninspirational departures since that of Pvt. Fleming in *The Red Badge of Courage*. Without dramatic gestures or fanfare, he makes the occasion seem antiheroic. Wearing his white stocking cap, Leper takes leave of his schoolmates, going into the army to find what he hopes will be a "recognizable and friendly face to the war." Leper represents to Gene what the entire class was seeking, a comprehensible way to cope with the violence of war. Only Finny, being shut out of this prospect, pays no attention to his classmates, who have projected Leper into a mythic figure like Kilroy, found everywhere in every theater of war: Leper is reputed to be behind the plot to kill Hitler; he is the liberator of North Africa; he is the bomber of the Ruhr dams; and he is responsible for the sinking of the German battleship *Scharnhorst*. As the first—and least likely—member of the senior class to go to the service, Leper is the class of 1943's liaison with World War II. The boys pretend that every allied victory is attributed to Leper in a joking way, but underneath their jest lurks a false bravado. Thus, when Leper cracks, it is like a bell tolling for all the boys, who are confronted with the possibility that it could happen to them.

Only Finny refuses to participate in the legend of Leper that is incremented with each new installment of war news. It is as though Finny alone understands that Leper is a kindred spirit of pacifism who, as he says, would not be able to shoot Hitler if he had a pistol at his temple. Finny's stance against the reality of the war is unshaken, and he prevails with Gene to disengage himself from the boys who go to the Butt Room to smoke and embellish on Leper's triumphs. Because of Phineas's influence, Gene finds himself drawn away from the rumors of war into a world inhabited by just "himself and me, where there was no war at all" (119). One cannot miss the irony of the situation here, where one group entertains illusions of war while the other is devoted to an illusion of peace.

In the face of the encroaching war, represented by Leper enlisting in the army, Finny devotes all of his energy to repudiating the reality of the world situation by organizing a winter carnival, the crowning endeavor of Finny's career at Devon. As the master of these revels, Finny's role as a "prince of peace" is seen most completely. In this episode Phineas's exertions take on mythic aspects. The return of the life force in the depths of winter is a deeply felt human need, particularly in the midst of a late winter in New England, when the world seems in frozen hiatus, the snow has lost its novelty and turned into dirty slush and frozen wind, and the sky has turned an "empty hopeless gray" that seems to be its "eternal shade"—then winter seems to have totally "conquered, overrun and destroyed everything" and there is "no longer any resistance movement left in nature" (120). Against an opponent, Finny takes the offensive against all negative elements in human life and nature. Undaunted, he represents the life force amidst the desolation; he declares a time to rejoice and opens the games of winter. Knowing no depressing weather and admitting no war in his philosophy, Finny has the spirit to introduce a spark of vitality into the dreary round of life at Devon. The centerpiece of the proposed Winter Festival, which will be staged in a park beside the ugly Naguamsett river, will be sports—ski jumps, slalom races, skating—all accompanied by music, food, and drink in the form of hard cider.

The ingenious spontaneity of Finny's plan is infectious. Even the legalistic Brinker is willing to turn rebel and break the rules against unsponsored events and enlists his service as festival supervisor. Like Gene, the bellicose Brinker seems disarmed by Finny's efforts; he, again like Gene, was on the brink of throwing himself to the destructive forces of war, but now that Gene has given his alliance to the fancy that the war is only something alleged by adults, Brinker has begun a long decisive sequence of withdrawals as his lessening commitment to the war is undercut by Finny's "choreography of peace," which reaches an apogee in the carnival festivities.

It is Finny, however, who is the controlling force behind the events of this day. Sitting like a potentate behind a large seminar table in the middle of the snowscape, looking, as Knowles comically describes it, like a "dowager in a saloon," Finny holds court from his ornately carved chair of heavy walnut adorned with the figures of lions' heads. The Olympic motif is suggested by statues in the form of effigies of various faculty, the school-dietitian, always a figure of scorn at boarding schools, and Hazel Brewster, the local "professional town belle." The unfolding of events that follow is handled in a Popean mock-burlesque manner. Rather than Grecian calm and moderation as Brinker "the law-giver" desires, all government breaks down and anarchy prevails. The decorous Brinker's mouth is plugged by Gene with a bottle of cider—a scene that is described metaphorically as a rape, with Brinker claiming that he had been "violated" (127). Intoxicated by the fumes of the hard cider, the boys offer up a sacrifice to the gods in ancient Olympic fashion by burning a treasured copy of Homer's *Iliad* containing a "pony." One of the boys, Chet Douglass, becomes inspired with his trumpet and pours out redemptions of classical, flamenco, and Dixieland jazz notes. Even Finny forgets his lameness and dances a jig on top of the table. Gene imagines himself soaring off the ski jump, although it is only a slight slope.

At this moment, at the apogee of Finny's influence, Gene says "his own inner joy at life for a moment as it should be, as it was meant to be in his nature, Phineas recaptured that magic gift for existing primarily in space. . . . It was his wildest demonstration of himself, of himself in the kind of world he loved" (128). During the final stages of the games, Gene is crowned with a wreath of evergreen boughs for the feats in the decathlon that include such outlandish stunts as walking on his hands upside down in a circle and balancing on his head atop the Prize Table. For this miraculous moment, Gene has acquired the perfect poise that Finny once had; under the benevolent influence of Phineas, all his "schoolboy egotism" is "conjured away" and Gene is liberated from the grim reality of external circumstances, symbolized by the gray weather and the world war, the outcome of which was by no means certain in the winter of 1943. Yet for this moment, Finny's illusions are infectious and for "this afternoon," at least, the boys of winter are able to achieve a "momentary, illusory, special and separate peace" (128).

Yet the fancy cannot cheat so well. As in a Greek drama, a messenger arrives on stage bearing bad news—in this case a telegram from Leper who has gone AWOL from the army and desperately seeks Gene's help.

Chapter 10 is the only section of the novel that takes place entirely outside the *mise-en-scène* of the schoolboy world. In this episode Gene undertakes a nocturnal pilgrimage to Leper's home in Vermont, where he comes closer than ever to the consequences of war. As Gene will discover, Leper has had a mental breakdown as a result of the traumatic experiences during basic training camp. The trip to Vermont, where even the homes seem afflicted from the freezing weather, is (as the mature voice of the narrator says) a portent of his own wartime experience, which entailed neither fighting nor marching, but monotonous nighttime journeys across the country from one military post to another as, "We were shuttled around America in pursuit of a role to play in a drama which . . . now had too many actors" (130).

Gene's perception at this point is that of his adult self, and it stands in contrast to the naive assumptions the younger Gene holds about his friend's plight. Since Leper had indicated in his wire only that he had "escaped" and needed help, Gene is puzzled by the odd choice of language. He cannot visualize how Leper would be an escapee, since he was in the army and not overseas. He comes to the rather illogical conclusion that Leper has escaped from foreign spies. This theory, although as preposterous as some of the imagined intrigues of Leper concocted in the Butt Room, gives Gene some measure of relief, something to believe in about the war, and a sense of pride that his friend is involved in a daring exploit involving espionage. Gene's fantasy glorifying the war and Leper is as misconceived, however, as Finny's illusion that there is no war, and the confrontation with Leper will dispel both. Upon arriving in Leper's hometown in upstate Vermont, Gene must walk out in the keen winds and brilliant sunlight to the rural house where his friend lives. It is described as a "brittle-looking" home, which aptly characterizes Leper as well. As Gene approaches, there is an incongruous sight. In one window hangs a small red, white, and blue flag with one star on it, indicating a son in military service, but in another window on ground level he sees Leper's face peering out. As Gene discovers, Leper has deserted from the army and taken refuge with his mother. The one-star flag, hung out so proudly by his patriotic mother, is mocked by the grim face of her fugitive soldier son.

In his conversation with Leper, Gene learns immediately that "spies" are not the cause of the trouble. Leper has been reduced to a near-psychotic condition by the pressures of military life. The dining room has become Leper's sanctuary because it is the only place where he can figure out what to do, and "not wonder what is going to happen." The three meals his mother serves him there can be counted on. Mechanical routines and functional acts such as eating have become a psychological crutch to him. At first Gene attempts false humor and uses a hearty tone, but his efforts fall flat. The seriousness of Leper's condition is made apparent by his confession that he has gone AWOL in order to avoid being discharged as psychologically unfit for military service. Leper's revelation of his condition to Gene leads to a clash of wills. Leper, sensitive to Gene's disdain of him, turns on him with an accusation; he tells Gene that he has always felt that Gene was "a savage underneath" and reveals that he knows it was Gene who knocked Finny out of the tree. As if to confirm Leper's accusation, Gene springs forward and knocks Leper out of his chair, spilling him onto the floor, where he curls up in a fetal position, alternately laughing and weeping hysterically.

It is important to understand Gene's reaction here. Leper has brought home an ugly truth to Gene—the violent side of his nature that is "underneath" his outward "nice" self. His remark revives Gene's sense of guilt, so far still suppressed. Gene's encounter with Leper is climactic for both of them. Gene is appalled at the sight of a person whose whole personality has collapsed. Whatever hope he had of helping Leper turns into an effort to maintain his own mental stability. Although Gene has physically assaulted Leper in his own home, he stays to take lunch because he is too "ashamed" to leave and because he feels he needs to know the full facts of Leper's case. Leper's mother is tacitly reconciled with Gene during the meal because he likes her cooking and, unlike Leper, eats with great appetite. Gene hopes that Mrs. Lepellier understands him, and her willingness to feed him and talk to him indicates that she knows he is a "good boy underneath" who regrets his lack of self-control. But, in a judgmental aside, the narrator says that Leper was closer to the truth about Gene's nature, showing that Gene now truly understands himself; at this point, however, he has not yet faced up to that fact.

During a walk across the snow-covered landscape following lunch, Leper reveals what has caused his crackup. Gene hopes that the frigid, natural scene will have a stabilizing effect on Leper, and he has a momentary illusion that Leper could not be "psycho" in the midst of the wintery outdoors that he loved. Yet, the crusty snow that crackles underfoot has ominous implications and seems to symbolize the fragility of the states of mind of both boys. In his treatment of Leper, Knowles shows a keen insight into disordered mental states; in this tautly drawn scene he reveals several interesting points that bear on Leper's condition. Most important, the nature of Leper's insanity seems to stem from fantasies of sexual transformation. In one instance, he is joking about Brinker's face on Snow White's body (which is the second time that Brinker has been the subject of a joke about his sexuality) and then he breaks down, sobbing and confessing to Gene that his psychological problem stems from his imagining a man's head on a woman's body or imagining inanimate objects like a chair's arm turning into a human arm. The experience with army life has been a phantasmagoria for Leper, during which everything was turned inside out. He reached a breaking point because he lost contact with the real identities of the people around him; he went crazy after he imagined that an uncommissioned officer changed into a woman. The account of Leper's confused sexual orientation is more than Gene can stand, maybe because at some level of his mind it reveals his confusion about his own sexual identity. Gene's own stability, like the frozen crust of snow he stands on, is in danger of cracking, so he runs away, disavowing any connection between what has happened to Leper and himself. Leper's psychological disintegration is nevertheless disturbing to Gene precisely because it bears so directly on his own struggle. Both Gene and Leper have attempted to avoid the reality of unpleasant facts, which Leper has escaped by going insane and which Gene has not yet faced up to. Thus, he strikes out at Leper first and then flees because he cannot accept the truth that he also has an irrational side to his being that he cannot control any more than Leper can prevent his mind from projected and disjointed sexual illusions. Gene's protest that Leper's case has "nothing to do with me" is highly ironic, because Gene is very much afraid that he too might not be able to stand the pressure of the war within that he fights alone or the stress of the war without that he will have to fight when his time comes.

Thus, the tenth chapter is a pivotal point in the novel. Knowles pushes closer here to the central theme of the novel—the presence of a blind, insane, ignorant evil in the heart of man that creates fear and causes hatred and destruction. Leper, with the unerring insight often found in the insane, probes Gene's conscience with his accusations and makes a private judgment on him that Gene will eventually have to acknowledge publicly. Leper's experience has forced him to "admit things" to himself; he understands that the same brutal forces that cause wars and necessitate armies are also present under the veneer of Gene's "good guy" personality. Gene, however, cannot accept Leper's wisdom of woe and rejects the whole of his experience, although Leper's problem—establishing a person's true identity—is ironically the same kind of identity crisis that Gene faces.

Hence, the episode in Vermont heightens the novel thematically as well, preparing for the subsequent culmination of events in the last three chapters, in which the tragic climax of the novel will turn on the reappearance of Leper. But this chapter is also remarkable for the quality of its writing, if for no other reason. Almost every word, sentence, and image has a sureness and rightness that only the best prose achieves. From the nighttime train trip to the description of rural Vermont, every physical detail is observed with perfect accuracy as well as being endowed with metaphorical implications. For instance, the train ride through the night, which, as we have seen, is a harbinger of Gene's own experiences in a seemingly mindless military bureaucracy, is written to convey psychologically the sense of time being telescoped by the acceleration of events. But it is in Knowles's treatment of weather in this chapter that he is most successful in communicating subtle psychological experiences, in the strikingly impressionistic handling of the final scene, in which Gene leaves Leper alone in the frozen snowfields. It is Gene's second act of betrayal of a friend in the novel, and as he flees from Leper, the sounds of the cold cracking the limbs of trees remind him of "distant rifle fire," suggesting metaphorically the parallel between a Gene abandoning his schoolmate and a frightened soldier deserting the battlefield in a panic. As Peter Wolfe remarked in an article on the impact of A Separate Peace, "Gene's failure here is one of moral escapism . . . Leper's description of the ugliness and disjointedness of life strikes Gene so hard that he must deny it in order to keep peace with himself."[35]

Those who have seen the film version of A Separate Peace may recall that the director altered some aspects of the plot in the situation between Gene and Leper. Instead of having Gene kick Leper out of his chair, he has Gene deliver a vicious blow to Leper's mouth outdoors in the snow where he falls to the ground and curls up in the fetal position, the red blood flowing from his mouth and making a stark contrast with the white snow. Rather than running away, as in the novel, Gene merely stands helplessly over his fallen friend as the camera pulls back, leaving them both diminished and helpless-looking in a setting of cold white bleakness. Although this is a deviation from the text, it is visually much more dramatic and is one of the most vivid moments in the film.[36]

The next two chapters of the novel describe the trial scene and Finny's second fall—events that lead up to the novel's tragic climax and prepare for the denouement, or final unravelling, of the plot in Chapter 13. As we have seen in the previous scene, the security of

Devon, with its comforting illusions of a world at peace, is the creation of Phineas, whose view of conflict is limited to athletics. Gene's first sight of Finny upon his return sharply contrasts with his last glimpse of Leper: he finds his friend in the middle of a snowball fight. The childish activity and boyish joy in life it expresses are a world away from the adult conflict that led to Leper's mental crippling. Although Finny too has been wounded by the evil inherent in life, he has not let his spirit be blighted. He is, as Gene knows, the organizing principle behind the snowball fight. Although it is an outlandish idea, he has succeeded in getting the top boys of the senior class to engage in the fray, which takes place on the most remote part of the campus on grounds, called "The Fields Beyond." Knowles here, as he does frequently throughout the novel, brings in a description of the physical background and gives it a metaphysical dimension. In this case it is onto the landscape that Gene wistfully projects his most deeply felt desire for a sanctuary from the mounting tension of his inner conflict. Standing on the edge of the woods watching Finny, Gene thinks that the trees represent something "primevally American, reaching in unbroken forests far to the north, into the great northern wilderness" and he wonders "whether things weren't simpler and better at the northern terminus of these woods, a thousand miles due north into the wilderness, somewhere deep in the Arctic, where the peninsula of trees which began at Devon would end at last in an untouched grove of pine, austere and beautiful" (144).

In a retrospective aside, the narrator confides to the reader that he now knows there is "no such grove," but at that point in his life he imagined that it might be "just over the visible horizon." After his confrontation with Leper's insanity and the reexposure to the ugly truth of his own guilt, Gene's mind is deeply disturbed, and his need to return to Phineas and Devon is a reaction to the disorder and irrationality experienced during his mission to help Leper—which, paradoxically, has helped Leper very little but has provided Gene with an additional perspective on himself and a glimpse into the "heart of darkness." Gene, like Marlowe in Conrad's great short novel about madness and depravity, is almost overcome by the vision of evil that he has witnessed, and he wants to insulate himself from anything disturbing. Thus, he seeks the same, ordered, Greek-inspired world Finny inhabits, a world that follows Olympian ideas and gives the prize to those soundest in body and spirit. Hence, he also sees the Devon woods in terms of the Edenic innocence that Finny represents. Life to Gene has become a "tangled" business, and the more he experiences existence beyond the groves of academe, the more he would like to evade it.

Gene's observations of Finny make up the rest of this scene and deserve comment. For instance, this scene is the last one in the novel where the reader sees Finny in his natural sphere—the world of games. Earlier we were given a lengthy description of Finny playing blitzball, and now Knowles provides us with a second look at Finny in his personal world of athletic competition. The activity takes place as winter is about to give way to spring, but there is still enough snow on the ground to make snowballs. In another passage of fine descriptive writing, Knowles creates one of the most unusual but evocative *reverdies* in literature. It is not that first robin, the usual herald of spring in New England, but the smell of the boys' clothing that reminds Gene of spring. Knowles writes, "Everywhere there was the smell of vitality in clothes, the vital something in wool and flannel and corduroy which spring releases. I had forgotten that this existed, this smell which instead of the first robin, or the first bud or leaf, means to me that spring has come" (146). Paradoxically, the odor from these sturdy winter garments not only gives Gene happiness, because with it is the promise of new vitality and energy as the land revives after winter, but it also creates in his mind an uncertainty about the future and the sort of clothing he might wear in future springs, when he must change from civilian clothes to khaki.

This scene suggests the actual wartime combat awaiting many of the "combatants" in the mock fight, who are described as the "cream of the school, the lights and leaders of the senior class . . ." (145). Now, however, their commanding general is Phineas, and, despite being crippled and in a cast, his movements and coordination are hardly impaired, only noticeable now because his earlier grace had been so perfect. The point on which Knowles wants the reader to focus here is the unique way Finny plays games. He keeps changing sides in the fight, going over to the side that needs help, "betraying" his side to "heighten the disorder" and to keep one group from defeat or victory because, as Gene realizes, "no one was going to win or lose;" the fight was a game in which the main thing to Finny was the action, not the outcome. In sports as in life for Finny, the important thing is not the end but the means, hence his dedication to activities like blitzball, swimming, and jumping from trees that are invented forms of play, outside of the sanctions of organized sports, and, above all, games where no score is kept. People like Finny who do not play by the usual rules are the one whom life breaks, as Hemingway wrote, and although Finny, perhaps thinking of another metaphor from *A Farewell to Arms,* would like to think that the bone is "supposed to be stronger when it grows together over a place where it's been broken once" (147), his case will prove the exception to the rule.

Just as the previous chapter was filled with portent for Gene, Chapter 11 contains many events that foreshadow Finny's fate. Gene, for instance, is alarmed by Finny's disregard for his injured leg during the snowball fight and reminds him that Dr. Stanpole had warned him to be careful not to fall again. Perhaps more ominous than all is that here Finny comes to terms with a truth that he has previously denied, the existence of a world at war. The revelation of Leper's experiences punctures Finny's willing suspension of disbelief about the war: "he quietly brought to a close all his special inventions which had carried us through the winter. Now the facts were reestablished, and gone were all the fantasies, such as the Olympic Games for A.D. 1944, closed before they had ever been opened" (150).

There are two other scenes here that touch on the theme of war and also reveal how the illusions held by Gene and Finny over the winter were only temporary stays from historical reality, a reality that both boys, if they were honest with themselves, have known all along. As the school year moves into its final phase with the approach of spring and graduation for the senior class, the campus is host to many military officers, who speak to the students about the merits of their services. To Gene the various military programs that are set up on college campuses, such as the navy's V-5 and V-12 programs and the army's Special Training Program, appear more and more attractive because they seem very safe, peaceful and "almost like just going normally on to college." So, rather than choosing a university, as would have been the case in peacetime, the Devon class of 1943 is faced with the decision of which branch of the military to choose. The normal crisis for prep school students in this year is not where they will attend college; rather, it is where they will go to be prepared for the final battles of the war. As Gene says, "There was no rush to get into the fighting; no one seemed to feel the need to get into the infantry . . . The thing to be was careful and self-preserving. It was going to be a long war" (151).

Gene's appraisal of himself and his classmates at this point reveals a retrospective wisdom, arising from a mature reflection on the events of his life, as he approaches his eighteenth birthday. However, in this stoic acceptance of the inevitable, we find an indication of a more composed and adult attitude. Gene is ready to accept his military responsibility, but he does not have any patriotic fantasies about war now. In an astute observation on the difference between the two worlds, military and the academic, that have been forced into an awkward collaboration by circumstances, Knowles writes, "Devon was by tradition and choice the most civilian of schools, and there was a certain strained hospitality in the way both the faculty and students worked to get along with the leathery recruiting officers who kept appearing on the campus . . . we could feel a deep and sincere difference between us and them, a difference which everyone struggled with awkward fortitude to bridge. It was as though Athens and Sparta were trying to establish not just a truce but an alliance—although we were not as civilized as Athens and they were not as brave as Sparta" (151).

The military theme and classical allusions are carried over into another scene that centers on Gene and Finny and shows two important sides of Phineas's character: his love of music and his distrust of conventional wisdom. Remember that Finny was first shown in this chapter doing something he loved—playing games—and when he next appears he is seen singing "A Mighty Fortress Is Our God." The insertion of this hymn being sung by Finny serves an important but subtle function. It reminds us that the ultimate protection and sanctuary from evil are not manmade military machines but rather something within the human heart. It is the force of the spirit that will, as the hymn goes, "Of mortal ills prevailing". Paradoxically, Finny, who has such great physical rhythm, is tone deaf and can't carry a tune; nevertheless, he loves all music profoundly.

The war theme appears in this chapter in the scene where Gene helps Finny with a Latin translation. The homework passage deals with "a surprise attack" on the Romans by the Gauls who ambush Caesar's legions in a swamp. Although Finny doubts if Gene's rather free translation will satisfy the literal-minded Latin teacher, he voices even greater doubt about the authenticity of Caesar, Rome, and the Latin language. He sweeps aside the whole concept of the reality of the events of two thousand years in the past. As emphatically as Huckleberry Finn, who discounted the Old Testament story of Moses by saying he did not take any "stock" in dead folks, Finny cannot accept a dead language, a dead empire, or a dead tyrant as facts that bear on the reality of his own existence. Books and teachers are also cynically regarded by Finny as conspirators who perpetuate historical illusions to keep the youth enslaved to remote facts. In another moment of candor, such as the earlier declaration of his friendship to Gene on the beach, Finny confesses to his roommate that it is important for him to believe in something. He adds, "I've got to believe in you, at least. I know you better than anybody" (155). Of course, this statement is dramatically very ironic, and again Gene is not capable of making an adequate or honest response. At this point, Finny's pretense that the war is a hoax has to be admitted, since he has no choice but to believe Gene's account of Leper's crackup. In addition, he too has seen the frightened Leper hiding in the bushes near the school chapel, and he says, "I knew there was a real war on," to which Gene replies, "Yes, I guess it's a real war all right, but I liked yours a lot better" (156). The boys have now come to the end of what Knowles equates to a "binge" of the imagination; they feel half-guilty but mutually amused, as cohorts who lived through an intoxicating experience and must now

resume more decorous deportment. In their last moment of com-
raderie before the revelation of Gene's secret, "the sun was doing
antics among the million specks of dust hanging between us and casting a brilliant, unstable pool of light on the floor" (156). Incidentally,
this intimate scene recalls the situation of shared light used to symbolize the symbiotic relationship in Chapter 4, where Finny sits opposite
Gene at the study table with the lamp casting "a round yellow pool
between us" (43). The light is indeed fading, and the momentary stay
against the truth that Gene and Finny had maintained over the better
part of the school term is about to end. The fragile stability of the
situation is shattered by the arrival in their room of Brinker at 10:05,
who announces that a court of inquiry has been convened to get to the
bottom of what happened at the tree.

The trial scene that follows is the final episode of this chapter and
precipitates the tragic catastrophe of the novel. Of all of the plot events
in the novel, this one has seemed most problematical to commentators,
who raise objections to the night court situation as a means to move
the story to a conclusion. Although Knowles has tried to prepare for
the kangaroo court by the earlier Butt Room inquiry into Gene's guilt
and has shown Brinker to be an unpleasant, oppressive sort of busy-
body full of veiled references to Gene's part in Finny's accident, our
understanding of the motives that lead Brinker to convene his court
are not adequate, because the point of view is restricted to Gene. Thus,
we never learn what Brinker is feeling or why he would so eagerly and
sadistically persecute his friend Gene. But perhaps more troubling to
most readers than Brinker's reasons for investigating the accident is
the tone of the court scene; it does not seem to be either a prank or
wholly serious. The uncertain feeling created by this scene caused the
movie makers trouble when they tried to recreate it for the film. Larry
Peerce, the director, attempted to make the atmosphere less horrible
and more comic by staging a parade of boys dressed in black who
stomped about singing an obscene song. He also shifted the scene from
the Assembly Room in the Academy Building to the Chapel to give the
mock tribunal of school boys the air of a priestly inquisition. Most
film reviewers found Peerce's treatment of this scene to be as faulty

and inherently flawed as the fictional version of this episode. To heighten the visual interest here, the two boys on trial were shot in close proximity to each other, both sharing the spotlight, as they had in earlier scenes been caught in pools of shared light.[37] Furthermore, this treatment adds to the two-as-one motif that the novel has developed throughout. But what the movie as well as the book lacks at this juncture is the sense of interior knowledge, which the character who is motivating the action could provide. Even with a prior knowledge of the novel's treatment of this scene, it is not fully comprehensible because we don't learn enough about the pretrial machinations of Brinker. There has been no previous indication that Brinker is concerned enough about the unsolved mystery of Finny's fall to go to the lengths that he does to solve it. Neither his dedication to facts nor his notion that Gene is spoiling Finny seems enough to warrant such an elaborate kangaroo court.[38]

It is, of course, now a mute question whether Knowles could have found a less contrived situation than the trial to bring about the revelation of the full truth of Gene's treachery to Finny. Yet, as the scene is written, it very effectively evokes a mood of gloom and impending doom. The windows have a "deadened look" about them; the walls appear opaque with blackened canvasses of deceased headmasters' portraits and a dead World War I hero, and the ten members of the senior class in black robes all create an ominous tone. At the beginning of the investigation both Gene and Finny express contempt for Brinker's court, but when Brinker brings up the matter of the accident and hints that it was not just a fall, Finny admits that he has had the same suspicion but never allowed himself to think about it, because he could accept the fact that Gene might have caused his injury. His confidence in Gene is shaken for the first time when Gene, under the pressure of Brinker's investigation, lies and claims that he was standing at the trunk of the tree, when Finny knows that he was with him out on the limb. The questioning turns to where Gene was, as Brinker refuses to believe that Gene cannot recall exactly where he was, and Finny, in a flash of recollection, cuts through to the truth, recalling that they climbed up the tree together to undertake a double jump. The members of the tribunal are not satisfied and demand a witness who can testify to the facts. Then Finny remembers that the AWOL Leper has returned to Devon and can clear up the matter, because he was also at the tree. Finny has suggested Leper as a witness no doubt because he hopes that he can clear Gene. Gene, on the other hand, hopes only that Leper will appear so deranged that no one will believe him, thus legally making him an unreliable witness. Much to Gene's chagrin, Leper looks quite well and his manner is composed and lucid.

Leper's testimony lays bare in vividly imagistic terms what actually took place at the tree. He tells the boys assembled that although the sun was in his eyes, he saw both Gene and Finny standing on the limb in a blaze of light from the setting sun, whose rays were "shooting past them like—like golden machine-gun fire" and that their silhouettes looked "black as death standing up there with all this fire burning all around them" (166). Although Leper is not able to make out who was who, he is able to say that that the person nearest the trunk of the tree bent his knees and pumped the branch in a pistonlike motion, causing the one out on the limb to fall. It is now clear to Phineas what happened, and he flees Assembly Hall, as if trying to evade the truth with a desperate physical gesture that would shake off the facts as he once shook off tacklers. The sound of his body tumbling down the marble staircase tells the others that he has taken a second terrible fall.

There are several salient features in the final and climactic scene that closes Chapter 11. As elsewhere in the novel, Knowles has employed imagery to define the emotional condition and thematic implications of this crucial situation. We have already commented on the images of death and darkness associated with the courtroom setting, but the imagery used by Leper in his testimony draws comparisons between the boys in the tree and men at war. If one remembers the opening description of the tree, it was associated with warfare, looking "as forbidding as an artillery piece." Here Leper's impressionistic creation of the moment of Gene's crime employs more war imagery—the sun's rays "shooting like golden machine gun fire"—thus linking what happens between the boys in the tree with the hostility of nations at war with each other.

CHAPTER 8

The Recovery: A New Life

In the aftermath of Finny's fall, there are a couple of suggestive descriptive details that Knowles adds to enhance the tragic dimensions of this event. First, the wounded Finny is depicted lying at the foot of the marble staircase "with light flooding down on him from the chandelier . . . isolated at the center of a tight circle of faces" (171). Then, as Finny is lifted into a chair to be taken to the infirmary, Gene notes, "People aren't ordinarily carried in chairs in New Hampshire, and as they raised him up he looked very strange to me, like some tragic and exalted personage, a stricken pontiff" (171). The image of Finny encircled by a ring of light and inquiring faces defines Finny's plight. He is totally immobilized and faces his final isolation in death, as the tightening of the ring of circumstances seals his fate. The image of Finny as high priest also defines his sacrificial role and points toward his tragic destiny. We think here of A.E. Housman's athlete, who, like Finny, dies too young and is chaired "by his comrades who take him away to become the townsman of a 'stiller town.' "

Chapter 12 contains the reconciliation between Gene and Finny and the coming to terms with the full facts about the fall, which had been resisted by both until Brinker's insistent crying out for the "f . . .

ing facts" with his court of inquiry. The trial ultimately reverses the implications of the first fall because it makes possible Gene's acceptance of his guilt and its full confession to Finny. As Finny's old wound has been opened, so has Gene's conscience been afflicted again by the full awareness of his guilt. So, while Finny suffers physical anguish, Gene undergoes an even more agonizing psychological disability, nearly going crazy himself.

At this point Gene's nerves are so taut and he is so distressed that he is almost hysterical. He fantasizes conversations between Finny and nurse "Windbag" and Dr. Stanpole, with his extensive vocabulary, in which Finny speaks only in Latin. Gene's mind and body are out of harmony, however, because thinking he is laughing, he is startled to discover that his face is wet with tears.

Gene's anguish is a result of his complete realization, for the first time, of the magnitude of his crime against his friend. As in earlier situations when the pangs of remorse grew too sharp, Gene has considered joining the armed forces to escape his guilt; for a moment he has an impulse to steal a car and run away, but instead he takes a midnight walk out across the campus and goes into the stadium. During this evening Gene undergoes a distorting psychological condition that causes him to lose contact with reality while experiencing a diminished sense of his own "epic grandeur which my superficial eyes and cluttered mind had been blind to before" (178).

As Leper had earlier found that he could not cope with reality and had retreated from it, so Gene's mind plays similar tricks on him. In his case, everything outside himself takes on a heightened reality as he loses his sense of identity, and he has the sensation that "my whole life at Devon had been a dream" and all the places and "people there were intensely real . . ." (178). Gene feels that he is excluded from this "solid and deeply meaningful world." This episode marks the nadir of Gene's isolation; his soul is lost and only Finny can restore it.

After spending all night in the stadium, Gene returns to school and finds a note from Dr. Stanpole instructing him to bring Finny's personal items to the infirmary. This meeting between Gene and Finny is their final one, and for Gene it is his chance to atone for his sin. In this very poignant scene, Gene faces up to the truth about the dual nature of everything in the world.

Gene is very apprehensive about seeing Finny again, since being rebuffed the night before when he tried to speak to him through the window of his infirmary room. A sensation of *déjà-vu* comes over Gene; he feels that he is reliving the events of the previous August when he had gone the first time to visit Finny in the infirmary. But Gene is more experienced now and is less shocked by violence because "there were hints of much worse things around us now . . . the news-reels and magazines were choked with images of blazing artillery and bodies half sunk in the sand of a beach somewhere" (179). Gene rationalizes that with the war so close to the members of the senior class as they neared graduation, Finny's broken leg would not seem so horrible. With these thoughts, Gene attempts to calm himself before his confrontation with Finny. This is the moment that the novel has been leading up to since the first fall from the tree. Gene's two earlier attempts to confess his part to Finny had failed, the first because Gene could not bring himself to a full confession, and the second at Finny's house where he had been unable to explain for fear of hurting his friend even more. At this point no further injury can be done, and Phineas and Gene can no longer evade the revelation of the full facts.

In this emotionally packed situation, Knowles writes with re-straint and avoids the excessive sentimentality with which hospital scenes are often treated. In dialogue that is tense and meaningful, he conveys the heightened atmosphere that surrounds the final meeting of Gene and Finny.

Gene, seeing that Finny is as tense as he is, starts to talk, explain-ing that he had already tried to confess and had come to visit him the night before because he thought that he belonged with Finny. This remark satisfies Finny that Gene is telling the truth, and his face regis-ters "a settled, enlightened look." Finny proceeds to make a confession to Gene that he has been deceiving him about his belief that there was no war. All along he has been trying to enlist in some branch of the armed forces but without success. Gene's response to Finny's admis-sion that he has been trying to get into the war while denying its existence is a summarizing statement that puts Finny's character into the fullest focus. Gene says, "Phineas, you wouldn't be any good in the war, even if nothing had happened to your leg . . . They'd get you some place at the front and there'd be a lull in the fighting, and the next thing anyone knew you'd be over with the Germans or the Japs, asking if they'd like to field a baseball team against our side . . . You'd get things so scrambled up nobody would know who to fight any more" (182).

In Gene's estimate, Finny's innocence so totally represents the spirit of peace that his very presence would make war appear unacceptable. His good will and fundamental idealism would overcome the fear and hostility that fuel war between men. Finny is moved by the honesty of Gene's tribute and in turn is willing to accept that Gene acted against him from a "blind impulse" rather than "anything you really felt against me" (183). Now that he comprehends that Gene behaved instinctively in a weak moment. Finny can forgive Gene as long as he believes that it was not a premeditated or personal motive that led him to commit his act of treachery. Gene is able to satisfy Finny by his final words that he does not hate him, saying, "It was just some ignorance inside me, some crazy thing inside me, something blind, that's all it was" (183). This statement amounts to an epiphany on Gene's part, for it reveals his discovery that the evil in himself is part of the universal corruption. In their last conversation, Gene has grown through his own suffering, to the point where he can reciprocate Finny's loving and honest nature, something he had heretofore been incapable of. Both he and Finny can accept what happened, if they can understand it as an animosity that is a consequence of human weakness. Thus, in a sense the fall has been a fortunate one, for it has led to self-discovery, making possible Gene's realization of his own true identity. It is, however, Finny's forgiveness that finally makes Gene's salvation possible and gives him the chance to redeem himself during the second stage of his life.

The cost of Gene's struggle for self-knowledge is extremely high, and the price for it is no less than Finny's life. Despite Dr. Stanpole's assurance that the injury to Finny's leg is a "clean break" and creating expectations that he will recover, when the leg is reset some bone marrow gets into the blood stream, and Finny dies of heart arrest. Trying to communicate his sympathy to Gene, the doctor explains: "There are risks, there are always risks. . . . An operating room and a war" (185) are much the same he suggests.

As unexpected as Finny's death is to the reader, it has been anticipated by Knowles and is indeed almost inevitable. The symbolism of Finny's broken heart is inescapable. He did not have the heart to keep up the illusion of the world that had sustained him. Finny's death is also necessary for Gene to achieve his eventual separate peace and to accept the understanding of himself that he learned from Finny. When Gene says that he did not weep at Finny's funeral, it is because he does not feel separated from his friend but instead feels so fully integrated that he says, "I could not escape a feeling that this was my own funeral, and you do not cry in that case" (186).

In the last chapter Knowles moves the plot forward several months to June 1943, when the class graduates. His purpose for extending the story beyond the dramatic point of Finny's death is to introduce the war theme again and to sound the generation gap motif. To do so he brings in a new character, Brinker's father, a World War I veteran whose "Nathan Hale" patriotism is offensive to both his son and Gene. His view of war is analogous to preparing one's résumé. Combat duty, according to Mr. Hadley, will provide war memories to reminisce about in future years as they recall their heroic youth in the marines, paratroops, or as frogmen. To Brinker and Gene the prospect of risking their lives in order to have some future bragging rights is totally unrealistic. Much to Mr. Hadley's dismay, Gene tells him he is going into the navy to avoid fighting in foxholes with the infantry; Brinker's plan is to join the coast guard because he hopes it will be a safer service. The scene, which is one of the only extended depictions of parents, with the exception of Leper's mother, is intended to draw a distinction between the older and younger generations. Paradoxically, the boys conclude that the World War I generation is childish and that they are the mature ones. Their disillusionment is akin to Finny's view, who maintained that the war was a joke that fat and foolish old men played on younger men. However,

Gene forms an independent idea. To him, "it seemed clear that wars were made not by generations and their special stupidities, but that wars were made instead by something ignorant in the human heart" (193). Nevertheless, the general attitude toward adults throughout the novel is derogatory, which perhaps explains one reason why *A Separate Peace* is such an appealing book to adolescent readers. As one critic has shown, the grownups in the novel are without exception depicted with disrespect.[39] Even their names sound derisive—Mr. Patch-Withers, Rev. Carhart, Dr. Stanpole, Mr. Prud'homme, Mr. Ludsbury, and Miss Windbag. All the authority figures are characterized by their inane or fatuous remarks, such as those made by the wrestling coach, Phil Latham, who hardly ever speaks except to say, "Give it the old college try," whether advising students about academic, social, religious, or sexual problems. On the other hand is the gabby but well-meaning Dr. Stanpole, who "talks in huge circles," recycling his million-word vocabulary. Besides the staff, there are the school masters like the unpleasant Mr. Ludsbury with his phony British accent and fondness for silly cracks like, "Has it been raining in your part of town?" Mr. Carhart, the chaplain, has an unreal outlook on the war that is revealed in his sermons about no atheists in foxholes, which move him to tears. None of these people is vicious, and Knowles is gentle in his satire, but there is not one single exemplary adult character in the cast. During their infrequent appearances, grownups are described by adjectives like "fat," "old," "fragile," "zany," "inane," and "grave." They are pink-cheeked like Mr. Hadley or florid-faced like Mr. Patch-Withers or else have unhealthy bellies like the old railroad man. The basic problem is that there is no meaningful communication between the younger and the older generation, and there are no adult role models for the boys. Even the army troops who take up billets in the school dormitories are not inspiring examples, and Gene's view of them is as derogatory as his attitude toward the teachers and other adults who are spoofed for their ineffectualness.[40]

The arrival of the Army Air Force parachute riggers detachment at Devon signals the end of all illusions of peace, as the civilian campus becomes a military installation "for the duration" of the war, as the phrase of the day went. Appropriately, the troops are quartered in the far common, the part of the school grounds that always seemed to Gene to be too new and a less essential part of Devon. Gene notes with bemused detachment the arrival of the troops from his room window. The soldiers do not look very bellicose to Gene in their rumpled khaki uniforms and straggling columns. They are singing a popular polka tune, "Roll Out the Barrel," and marching behind jeeps and trucks loaded with sewing machines rather than machine guns. The irony of the military occupation of troops who pack parachutes to insure safe falls is certainly intended in light of the one of the novel's major motifs—falling from trees and down stairs, as well as the fallen nature of man. The military occupation of Devon soon makes the campus unrecognizable as olive green trash barrels sprout and stenciled signs denoting military offices and areas appear everywhere, giving the school a changed atmosphere marked by a "conscious maintenance of high morale" (193).

The last pages of the novel serve to extend Gene's awareness as narrator beyond the moment in time that he is located and to assure us that he has reached the point of understanding his experiences. This part of the novel thus forms a kind of coda that conveys Knowles's evaluation of the book's meaning.

Gene's recovery and reintegration, which will cure his alienation and "double vision," depend upon a process of spiritual symbiosis. Those qualities in Finny that were most vital and life-giving are assumed by Gene, while the negative traits are exorcised by Finny's death. Gene's psyche is integrated and harmonized by the forgiveness and love that Finny extended to his friend. Thus, a transfigured Gene faces life in an atmosphere Phineas created, "sizing up the world with erratic and entirely personal reservations, letting its rocklike facts sift through and be accepted only a little at a time..." (194). In an estimate of Finny's character that is reminiscent of *The Great Gatsby*, Knowles writes, "He possessed an extra vigor, a heightened confidence in himself, a serene capacity for affection which saved him . . . Nothing even about the war had broken his harmonious and natural unity" (195). Paradoxically, as Gene listens to an army drill instructor calling cadence, he involuntarily gets into step with the count, in a way anticipating his transformation into military life. He says that "later under the influence of an even louder voice . . . I fell into step as well as my nature, Phineas-filled, would allow" (196).

Finny's friendship has taught Gene that instinctive and impulsive reactions to life need not be evil or savage. His life offered Gene the example of a positive possibility, an ideal of conduct that he can commit himself to follow. So when Gene goes off to the war, he goes without any hatred, and he never kills anyone because, as he says, "he has already killed his enemy"—meaning that he has eliminated self-ignorance, which was his real enemy. Thus, he has made a separate peace, and war within himself, which he had waged at such a high cost, is finally over.

CHAPTER 9

Final Reflections

John Gardner pointed out that novels that succeed with academic critics meet certain requirements. Such books are "well-made," all the symbols clicking together neatly. Moreover, the fiction reveals human limitations and teaches right behavior. Knowles's *A Separate Peace* certainly conforms to these criteria, especially the last. The book is, at its most profound level, a fable about flawed human nature. It takes up the preoccupation with original sin and the loss of innocence that starts in American literature with James Fenimore Cooper and runs through Hawthorne, Melville, and Henry James up to Fitzgerald and Faulkner, to name just a few. The act of a young boy's betrayal of his friend becomes a paradigm of the evil, fear, and ignorance that causes hostility between individuals. Knowles's purpose is to show this general human limitation through a particular case, which is the first of all the qualities of this interesting and moving story that engages the reader. Although a New England boys' school might seem to be an unlikely backdrop for a book whose themes are the loss of paradise and original sin, Knowles is following a long tradition in his study of the fall of man. As R. W. B. Lewis shows in his classic study of the theme of innocence, *The American Adam*, the new world introduced a new kind of hero in fiction: "an individual emancipated from history, happily bereft of ancestery, untouched and undefiled by the usual inheritances of family and race. . . ."[41] The American Adam, as one might expect in a new and optimistic culture such as ours, is usually the unfallen or innocent Adam. All these traits and more are contained in the character of Phineas, whose fate makes literal use of the theme of the fall; however, Knowles's use of Adamic imagery in *A Separate Peace* is ultimately hopeful. Gene through his relationship with Finny is able to repudiate his former self and assume aspects of Finny's nature that will permit him a second chance and leave him a lifetime in which to find a private atonement for the betrayal of innocence. The pattern of Christian symbolism and doctrine that underlies the structure of *A Separate Peace* has been noticed by numerous commentators and is confirmed by Knowles, who acknowledges that he was reared in a deeply religious family and consciously used biblical themes and images as he composed the novel.

An aspect of Knowles's fictional technique that has not yet been remarked upon is the use of descriptive names for the characters in the novel. Just as Knowles was careful with the larger symbolic structure, it seems certain that he chose the names of the two central characters with equal regard for their symbolic suggestion.

In the case of Gene (whose surname is Forrester), his given name is obviously a shortening of Eugene, from Greek meaning "wellborn," implying that the bearer of the name is generally clean and noble, or at least fortunate in health and antecedents. The idea behind the name ultimately derives from the word *eugenes,* from which comes "eugenics," the science that deals with the improvement of the hereditary qualities of individuals and races. The implications of Gene's name are apparent in light of his role in the book. He is the narrator as well as the protagonist. His growth and development vis-à-vis his relationship with Phineas provide the basic theme. Gene is the ambitious scion of a Southern family whose home is not precisely located but seems to be in Georgia. The Forresters, we presume, are well off or at least able to afford an expensive Eastern prep school for Gene. Thus, Gene's surname fits very well with his given name, because he does indeed appear to be a wellborn Southern aristocrat. Forrester is an English surname that can be traced back to the early Middle Ages, around the 1200s. It derives from the occupation or office of forester, the warden whose duty it was to protect the woods of a lord. The officer was an enforcer, keeper, and custodian. Thus, even Gene's last name suits his role in the novel because he literally becomes a "keeper," first of the dark secret of his guilty act, which crippled Finny; then he becomes keeper of Finny's athletic feats, by participating in his stead; and finally he keeps the faith in life that Finny has instilled in him.

It is not only in a social sense that Gene is well-born; he is also bright and good at sports, although not as good an athlete as his friend Finny. He appears to embody the Greek ideal of a sound mind in a sound body, *mens sana in corpore sano*. Gene's appellation also has an ironic aspect because he lacked much while he was growing up despite being wellborn. From the narrator's account of what he was like as a student at Devon School fifteen years earlier, we learn that he has improved a great deal since the summer of 1942. He has gotten over the fear that haunted him during those years, and he has come through World War II without any scars, either mental, moral, or physical. Gene says, "I began at that point in the emotional examination to note how far my convalescence had gone." As he walks across the campus, he notes the way the architecture blends together and wonders, "I could achieve, perhaps unknowingly already had achieved, this growth and harmony myself" (4).

He has at last come to terms with himself, yet his rehabilitation was due in no small part to Phineas. Thinking of what he owes his former friend, Gene says, "During the time I was with him, Phineas created an atmosphere in which I continued now to live . . ." (194).

The choice of the name Phineas even more fully satisfies the meaning of the character's role in the novel. In the first place, Phineas is one of those characters in literature and folk culture—like Tarzan, Shane, McTeague, and Beowulf—who has no last name, which calls attention to the given name and endows it with an added dimension. Secondly, the name Phineas is rare in the United States. Even in New England where it was a popular name through the Puritan period, it steadily died out in the eighteenth and nineteenth centuries, and would have been an extremely odd name in the 1940s.[42]

In literary history the name appears in the titles of two of Anthony Trollope's lesser-known novels, *Phineas Finn, the Irish Member* (1869) and *Phineas Redux* (1874). Jules Verne also gave the name Professor Phineas T. Fogg to his central character in *Around the World in Eighty Days*. There are literary antecedents for the name in Greek mythology as well, where many writers of antiquity—but most prominently Ovid in his *Metamorphosis*—mention a "Phineas" who was a soothsayer-king of Thrace. He was afflicted with blindness by Zeus, whom he angered by revealing the future of mortals. Other versions of the myth say Poseidon blinded Phineas for directing Jason and the Argonauts through the Clashing Rocks.

One must go to biblical history, however, to find the kernel of meaning that most applies to the character Phineas. In the Old Testament there are three figures named Phineas. The name means "oracle" in Hebrew or "mouth of brass" and is first mentioned in Exodus (Exod. 6:25). This Phineas, the son of Aaron, is a judge and priest; a devout keeper of the covenant with the Lord, he gave rise to a line of priests known as "the sons of Phineas." There is another Phineas, but he is not so exemplary. He is the youngest son of Eli, a rebellious youth who was a rulebreaker; he redeemed himself by protecting the Ark. The third individual in the Bible who has the name Phineas is an angel, and it is this figure who has the most bearing upon the Phineas in the novel.[43] In the book of Judges (Judg. 2:1) the youngest of the seventy-two angels of the Lord "who comes up from Gilad" is called Phineas. This angel's "countenance glowed like a torch when the light of the Holy Ghost rested upon it," says the Scripture. It is interesting to note that an angel is by definition a presence whose powers transcend the logic of our existence. Also, as St. Augustine wrote, "Every visible thing in this world is put under the charge of an angel."

It might be possible to make a tangential application of the careers of the first two biblical characters to the situation of Phineas in the novel, but it is the shared nature of the angel Phineas in the Bible and the boy Phineas in Knowles's book that will be examined.

Final Reflections

One cannot think that it is stretching a point to say that Gene has come to regard Phineas as his guardian angel. After Phineas has died Gene says, "[Phineas] was present in every moment of every day . . ." (194). He is convinced that his friend Finny has given him a standard of conduct and credo that will save him from the negative emotions created by a world at war. Finny shares numerous other angelic traits with his namesake. The angel Phineas was remarkable for his compelling voice and his face with glowing features. Phineas is described in the early chapters in remarkably similar terms. Gene says of his voice, "[It was] the equivalent in sound of a hypnotist's eyes" (6). And again, speaking of Finny, "He rambled on, his voice soaring and plunging in its vibrant sound box . . ." (14). Describing Finny participating in class discussions, Gene says, "When he was forced to speak himself the hypnotic power of his voice combined with the singularity of his mind to produce answers which were not often right but could rarely be branded as wrong" (40). In addition to a remarkable voice, Finny's glowing green eyes light up his face. When excited his green eyes widen and he has a maniac look; we are told that his "eyes flash green across the room and that he blazed with sunburned health" (14). In the longest description given of Finny's face, Gene notes his friend's odd appearance: "Phineas had soaked and brushed his hair for the occasion. This gave his head a sleek look, which was contradicted by the surprised, honest expression which he wore on his face. His ears, I had never noticed before, were fairly small and set close to his head, and combined with his plastered hair they now gave his bold nose and cheekbones the sharp look of a prow" (19).

When one reviews the peculiar physiognomy of Phineas as well as the suggestions raised by his hypnotic voice, vivid blue-green eyes (39), and his extrasensory hearing (11), it seems that the angelic parallel is inescapable. Angels traditionally are endowed with supernatural and seeming magic powers of voice and eye, which they use to enthrall their listeners; also, angels, according to medieval lore, have fine ears in order to hear the music of the spheres. Furthermore, the sleek, shiplike features of Phineas are in keeping with early Christian angel iconography, as is his skin, "which radiates a reddish copper glow"

(39). Finally, there is one more analogy that pertains here. Angels, according to the doctrines of the early church, were immortal but not eternal. Also, it was held possible for virtuous men to attain angelic rank. While no mention is made of Finny in the next world in *A Separate Peace*, it is apparent that he was an influence—if not a supernatural one, then a benevolent one—who, in the role of Gene's savior, plays the part of an angel in deed as well as in name.

It is not possible to say whether Knowles intended Phineas to be linked with precursors who bore this name in scripture and in myth, or with Christian legends of angels. It is, however, a matter of record that Knowles writes to challenge the reader. In an essay entitled "The Young Writer's Real Friends," he says, "I think readers should work more. I don't want to imagine everything for them." The names of both Gene and Finny, then, are aptly chosen; whether by design or "a grace beyond the reach of art," they seem to be perfectly natural and inconspicuous names on the literal level that also function symbolically, focusing through their interpretation the theme of the novel even more clearly.

Readers of *A Separate Peace* might be interested to know that Knowles wrote a sequel to his first novel entitled *Peace Breaks Out*, published by Holt, Rhinehart and Winston in 1981. While the new book depends on *A Separate Peace*, none of the characters from the first book appear. It does retain the Devon school as a setting and again uses the prep school as a microcosm to focus on the larger issues of human existence. As *A Separate Peace* concerns itself with a group of schoolboys trying to deal with the pressures of a world at war, *Peace Breaks Out* shows students at Devon trying to find a basis for life in a world after war. Knowles's point in the sequel is that peace can bring mixed blessings. The nation, having defeated all external enemies, now moves to eliminate all internal foes, real or imagined. Here the enemy is depicted as those who would corrupt the "Devon Spirit," which is obviously intended to parallel the paranoia that beset the country in the McCarthy era, when witchhunting government committees were seeking out cases of anti-Americanism.

The title of *Peace Breaks Out* is cleverly chosen and comes from Bertolt Brecht's mother courage, the camp-follower, who has stocked up on scarce goods that she plans to sell to soldiers and who is dismayed by the news that "peace has broken out," spoiling her scheme to turn huge war profits. Through the allusion in the title, Knowles suggests that even something as desirable as world peace is problematical for some. This is another point of his second Devon novel; peacetime itself can be a time when individuals have to adapt to new situations, and some will not be capable of making smooth adjustments.

A Separate Peace is essentially a morality play, and so is *Peace Breaks Out*. The book centers on Pete Hallam, the book's narrator. A young alumnus—class of 1937—he has returned to Devon to teach history after wartime service as a combat infantryman. The school, however, does not provide the restful haven he was seeking after the trauma of the battlefields of Europe. The new generation of students seems confused; they have been brought up to expect to fight a war and feel shortchanged because it is over; they are as uncertain of their future as before. They were too young for the war, but its violence and destruction have been impressed upon them. They are aware of the realities of history and know too soon that the world is not an innocent place.

The plot action revolves around the conflict between two students. A German sympathizer named Hochschwender is a blatant Nazi and racist, and his views make him the enemy of a boy named Wexford, a superpatriotic type who is intolerant of anyone with different views. As names were used in *A Separate Peace* for symbolic purposes, so is there a suggestion here that each boy's name is thematically incremental. Wexford's name, for instance, which is Anglo-Irish in origin, is indicative of the "waxing" or growing climate of intolerance in America of those who are perceived as different and thus dangerous. Hochschwender, on the other hand, is an obviously German name that suggests the term of a shunned person, a *Schuwnder*, which is intensified here by the suffix *hoch*, making the name a highly undesirable person. Thus, both boys bear names that by implication suggest their respective roles in the novel. The two boys, both in Pete Hallam's American history course, have heated exchanges in class over politics. Wexford, the editor of the school newspaper, heads a drive to have a stained-glass window put in the chapel as a war memorial.

When the window is smashed by vandals, the blame is laid on Hochschwender with no proof, and he is accidentally killed by an overzealous group of the top athletes at Devon who had been aroused by Wexford against him.

Peace Breaks Out is written in the same sparse style of *A Separate Peace*. It also has a skillfully constructed plot that evolves with the cycle of the seasons through the school year calendar. Like *A Separate Peace*, it deals with a serious theme—the power of intolerance and blind self-righteousness to overcome individuals and entire societies. Some reviewers felt that even though Knowles's intentions were of the highest order, the quality of his writing had slipped and there was a loss of control over his material. As with Knowles's other books since *A Separate Peace*, *Peace Breaks Out* does not match his early achievement, and he seems resigned to being both blessed and cursed by the success of his first effort at a novel. Each work that followed *A Separate Peace* has been compared unfavorably with it because, as Knowles says, readers of his later work have expected novels that resembled *A Separate Peace*. Although in *Peace Breaks Out* Knowles produced a "companion novel" to *A Separate Peace*, it is flawed by the same artistic weakness of most of Knowles's writing since *A Separate Peace*: the tendency to correlate outside historical forces and motivation of characters.

As one critic has noted, however, Knowles's best work shows a sensitivity to psychological struggles between love and enmity, between loyalty and freedom, between the need to accept guilt and the need to be absolved from it.[44] In *A Separate Peace*, Knowles admirably balanced the handling of the plot, character, and setting, creating a modern version of the fall from innocence. Any final assessment of Knowles's achievement must conclude with the acknowledgment that he is a writer of highly crafted prose, with a talent for capturing local atmosphere and a capacity for revealing the duality of the human heart. *A Separate Peace* is a work of fiction that tells a story that many people have felt was true for them on a deep emotional level. The book has influenced millions of readers already and will continue to do so. To have had this kind of response, if for only one book in a writing career, an author should take great pride.

Notes and References

1. John Knowles, *A Separate Peace* (New York: Dell, 1975), 32.

2. Studs Terkel, *The Good War: An Oral History of World War Two* (New York: Pantheon Books, 1984), 354.

3. John Knowles, "On *A Separate Peace*," *The Exonian*, 1 November 1972, 2.

4. Howard T. Easton, "Life in the Forties," *The Exonian*, 28 October 1972, 4.

5. H. D. Curran, "The Summer Session of 1942," *Phillips Exeter Alumni Bulletin*, 1942, 7–9.

6. Myron R. Williams, *The Story of Phillips Exeter Academy* (Exeter, N.H.: Exeter Publishing, 1957), 127–33.

7. *This Fabulous Century, 1940–1950*, vol. 5 (New York: Time-Life Books, 1969), 244.

8. Henry C. Herge, et al., *Wartime College Training Programs of the Armed Services* (Washington, D.C.: American Council on Education, 1948), 3–15.

9. John Knowles, "My Separate Peace," *Esquire*, March 1985, 107–9.

10. Knowles, "My Separate Peace," 109.

11. Knowles, "My Separate Peace," 107.

12. Knowles, "My Separate Peace," 108.

13. John Knowles, "Phineas," *Cosmopolitan* (May 1956), 74–79.

14. "Interview with Knowles," *New York Times* 8 October 1972, sec. 2, p. 21.

15. John Knowles, "A Turn with the Sun," *Story, The Magazine of the Short Story in Book Form*, no. 4 (1953); also in *Phineas: Six Stories* (New York: Random House, 1968), 3–27.

16. John Knowles, "A Naturally Superior School," *Holiday* 18 (December 1956): 70–72, 134–38.

17. Knowles, "Superior School," 73.

18. Knowles, "Superior School," 138.

19. Knowles, "Superior School," 138.

20. John Knowles, "A Protest From Paradise," *Art and the Craftsman: The Best of the Yale Literary Magazine 1836–1961*, ed. Joseph Harned and Neil Goodwin. (Carbondale: Southern Illinois University Press, 1961), 201–2.

21. Sister M. Nora, "A Comparison of Actual and Symbolic Landscapes in *A Separate Peace*," *Discourse* 11 (Summer 1968): 356–62.

22. John Knowles, "Interview with Editors of *Exonian*," *Exonian*, 1 November 1972, 2.

23. John Knowles, "The Young Writer's Real Friends," *The Writer* 75 (July 1962): 12–14.

24. James Ellis, "*A Separate Peace*: The Fall from Innocence," *English Journal* 53 (May 1964): 13–18.

25. Ian Kennedy, "Dual Perspective Narrative and the Character of Phineas in *A Separate Peace*," *Studies in Short Fiction* 11 (1967): 353–59.

26. Hallman Bryant, "Phineas's Pink Shirt in Knowles's *A Separate Peace*," *Notes on Contemporary Fiction* 15 (1984): 5–7.

27. Claire Rosenfield, "The Shadow Within: The Conscious and Unconscious Use of the Double," *Daedalus* 92 (1963): 338.

28. Rosenfield, "The Shadow Within," 339.

29. Paul Witherington, "*A Separate Peace*: A Study in Structural Ambiguity," *English Journal* 54 (1965): 795–800.

30. Witherington, "*A Separate Peace*," 795.

31. Leslie Fiedler. "The Eye of Innocence" in *No: In Thunder Essays on Myth and Literature* (New York: Stein and Daly, 1972), 281–82.

32. Fiedler, "The Eye of Innocence," 283.

33. George-Michael Sarotte, *Like a Brother, Like a Lover* (New York: Anchor Press/Doubleday, 1978), 45–46.

34. "Vibrations: An Interview with John Knowles about the Film 'A Separate Peace' " *Ingenue* 14 (1972): 20–21.

35. Peter Wolfe, "The Impact of Knowles's *A Separate Peace*," *University Review* 36 (1970): 197.

36. Linda Heinz, "*A Separate Peace*: Filming the War Within," *Literature Film Quarterly* 3 (1975): 168.

37. Heinz, "*A Separate Peace*," 167–168.

38. Heinz, "*A Separate Peace*," 169.

39. Sister M. Amanda Ely, "The Adult Image in Three Novels of Adolescent Life," *English Journal* 56 (1967): 1127–29.

40. Ely, "The Adult Image," 1130.

Notes and References

41. R. W. B. Lewis, *The American Adam* (Chicago: University of Chicago Press, 1955), 5.

42. G. R. Stewart, *The American Dictionary of Given Names* (New York: Oxford, 1979), 213.

43. Gusta Davidson, *A Dictionary of Angels* (New York: Macmillan, 1967), 224.

44. Robert M. Nelson, "John Knowles," in *Dictionary of Literary Biography—American Novelists since World War II,* second series (Detroit, Michigan: Gale Research Company, 1980), 177.

Bibliography

PRIMARY SOURCES

A Separate Peace, London: Secker and Warburg, 1959; New York: Macmillan, 1960.

Morning in Antibes. New York: Macmillan, 1960; London: Secker and Warburg, 1964.

Double Vision: American Thoughts Abroad. New York: Macmillan, 1964; London: Secker and Warburg, 1964.

Phineas. New York: Random House, 1968.

The Paragon. New York: Random House, 1971.

Spreading Fires. New York: Random House, 1974.

A View of Riches. Boston: Little, Brown, 1978.

Peace Breaks Out. New York: Holt, Rhinehart & Winston, 1981.

The Private Life of Axie Reed. New York: E. P. Dutton, 1986.

SECONDARY SOURCES

Alley, Douglas, "Teaching Emerson through *A Separate Peace.*" *English Journal* 70 (January 1981): 19–23. Shows how Knowles relies on Emerson's philosophy of friendship in *A Separate Peace* with parallel quotations from the novel and essays.

Bryant, Hallman B. "Symbolic Names in Knowles's *A Separate Peace.*" *Names* 34 (1986): 83–88. Deals with the onomastic function of the main characters' names and discusses their allegorical significance.

———. "Finny's Pink Shirt." *Notes Contemporary Literature* 15 (1984): 5–7. Traces of origin of pink shirt as fashion item.

Bibliography

Carragher, Bernard. "There Really Was a Super Suicide Society." *New York Times* 8 October 1972, sec. 2, pp. 2, 7, 17.

Crabbe, John K. "On the Playing Fields of Devon." *English Journal* 52 (1963): 109–11. Offers a brief survey of the novel's plot and recommends the use of the book to high school teachers as an alternative to *Catcher in the Rye.*

Devine, J. E. "The Truth About *A Separate Peace.*" *English Journal* 58 (1969): 519–20. Finds Finny to be in reality the villain of the book because of his "intrinsic aversion of art, beauty, justice, order, freedom, and democracy."

Ellis, James. "*A Separate Peace:* The Fall From Grace." *English Journal* 53 (1964): 313–18. Elucidates the three sets of symbols which provide the basic structure of the novel: the summer and winter terms; the Devon and Naguamsett Rivers; and peace and war, showing how the first pair of each set gives way as the plot progresses, ending with Gene's discovery that the spirit of innocence found in Finny is the best defense against evil.

Ely, Sister M. Amanda, O.P. "The Adult Image in Three Novels of Adolescent Life." *English Journal* 56 (1967): 1127–31. Finds a pattern of derogatory treatment of adults, who are shown as intolerant, insane, or ineffectual, and not exemplary role models for the adolescents.

Foster, M. P. "Levels of Meaning in *A Separate Peace.*" *English Record* 18 (1968): 34–40.

Greiling, Franziska Lynne. "The Theme of Freedom in *A Separate Peace.*" *English Journal* 56 (1967): 1269–72. Draws parallels between the Greek ideal of harmony and Finny's attitude toward life, which he transmits to Gene at the end of the novel.

Halio, Jay. "John Knowles's Short Novels." *Studies in Short Fiction* 1 (1964): 107–12. Appreciates the taut, spare style of Knowles' early novels, which have more to say about how man must come to terms with himself than many overly lengthy recent works.

Haniz, Linda and Roy Huss. "*A Separate Peace:* Filming the War Within." *Literature Film Quarterly* 3 (1975): 160–71.

Kennedy, Ian. "Dual Perspective Narrative and the Character of Phineas in *A Separate Peace.*" *Studies in Short Fiction* 11 (1967): 353–59. Compares Knowles's handling of the first-person narrator with Dickens's use of Pip as a narrator at younger and older stages of life in *Great Expectations.*

McDonald, James L. "The Novels of John Knowles." *Arizona Quarterly* 23 (1967): 335–42. Places Knowles's fiction in the tradition of the novel of manners, showing his affinities with Henry James and Scott Fitzgerald in choice of subjects, themes, and techniques.

McDonald, Walter R. "Heroes Never Learn Irony in *A Separate Peace.*" *Iowa English Bulletin Yearbook* 22 (1972): 33–36. Reads the conclusion of the novel in an ironic light. Gene's actions toward Finny in the episode at the tree were motivated by jealousy and hate. Throughout the novel, Gene is unable to face fully questions about human evil that remain hidden to him.

Mellard, James M. "Counterpoint and 'Double Vision' in *A Separate Peace*." *Studies in Short Fiction* 4 (1966): 127–34. This instructive essay discusses the method of counterpoised elements, even seen in the point of view Knowles employs to present a double perspective of events, setting, and characters, all of which bear out the duality that lies "at the very heart of human existence."

Mengeling, Marvin E. "*A Separate Peace*: Meaning and Myth." *English Journal* 58 (1969): 1323–29. Interprets the events of the novel as a mythic quest for the ideals of ancient Greece. Phineas represents Apollo and the sponsoring of the Winter Carnival is the Olympic spirit increased in him. He also takes on aspects of Dionysus, the god whose death gives new life.

Nelson, Robert McDowell. "Some Instances of Double Vision in Post-War Fiction: Essays of Knowles, Hawkes, and Barth." Ph.D. diss., Stanford University, 1975. Argues that the motif of duplication found throughout *A Separate Peace* controls the form of the novel and conforms to Knowles's vision that all human nature is divided into a best-self, worst-self antithesis.

Nora, Sister M. "A Comparison of Actual and Symbolic Landscape in *A Separate Peace*." *Discourse* 11 (1968): 356–62. Makes a careful study of the actual setting of the novel to compare reality with fictional locale. Concludes that Knowles combined, eliminated, and heightened the sites to suit his artistic purpose.

Pomeranz, Regina. "Self-Betrayal in Modern American Fiction." *English Record* 14 (April 1964): 21–28. Contends that Knowles, like other younger writers, does not just explore the consequences of self-betrayal, but shows the rejection of betrayal and search for honor.

Rosenfield, Claire. "The Shadow Within: The Conscious and Unconscious Use of the Double." *Daedalus: Journal of the American Academy of Arts and Sciences* 92 (1963): 326–44.

Sarotte, George-Michael. *Like a Brother, Like a Lover*. Garden City, N. Y.: Doubleday, 1978. Analyzes Gene's hatred of Finny as product of his fear of falling in love with his "virile ideal." His anxiety about his relationship with Finny is due to sexual maladjustment caused by suppressed homoerotic attraction.

Travis, Mildred. "Mirror Images in *A Separate Peace* and *Cat and Mouse*." *Notes on Contemporary Literature* 5 (1975): 12–15. Discovers parallels between the two novels in characterizations, plot action, and treatment of the myth of the fall from innocence, which in each case is raised from the local and specific situation and given universal significance.

Bibliography

Umphlett, Willey Lee. *The Sporting Myth and the American Experience: Studies in Contemporary American Fiction*. Lewisburg, Pennsylvania: Bucknell University Press, 1975. Relates Phineas to a type of American sporting hero, an archetypal figure that in literary treatments "passes from primal innocence to a complex fate."

Ward, Hayden. "The Arnoldian Situation in *A Separate Peace*." *Bulletin of West Virginia Association of College English* 1 (1974): 2–10. Develops a relevance between Arnold's poetry and Knowles's novel, both of which express feelings of subdued despair.

Weber, Ronald. "Narrative Method in *A Separate Peace*." *Studies in Short Fiction* 3 (1965): 63–72. Makes the point that Knowles in *A Separate Peace*, unlike Salinger in *Catcher in the Rye*, attempts a deliberate distance in point of view, which is handled with precise and economical craftsmanship. Modification of the first person narrative allows Gene to look back on his experience with a greater self-understanding than is possible to Holden Caulfield.

Witherington, Paul. "*A Separate Peace*: A Study in Structural Ambiguity." *English Journal* 54 (1965): 795–800. Attempts a broader interpretation of the tension between Gene and Finny by investigating the "ambiguous moral atmosphere" expressed in the characters, setting, and imagery of the novel. Gene learns to appreciate the variety and relativity of human existence as a result of what he experiences.

Wolfe, Peter. "The Impact of Knowles's *A Separate Peace*." *University Review* 36 (1970): 189–98. Examines the means by which Knowles poses the basic question of whether or not it is possible for humans to overcome our primal bestiality. Gene's struggle with the shadow of irrational hatred within him has not been overcome. Even after fifteen years, when he returns to the scene, he has not yet made his peace with the past.

Index

Index

Hemingway, Ernest: *A Farewell to Arms*, 1, 38, 97; *Nick Adams Stories*, 17
Hicks, Granville, 14–15
Holiday magazine, 12, 29
Housman, A. E., 103

James, Henry, 111

Kazin, Alfred, 16
Keats, John: "Ode to Autumn," 79
Kennedy, Ian, 42
Kilroy, 87
Knowles, John: Air Force Academy lecture, 60; *Exonian* interview, 31; *Ingenue* interview, 68; *New York Times* interview, 24; religious upbringing, 112; "Descent to Proselito," 32; "A Naturally Superior School," 28–30; *Peace Breaks Out*, 116–18; "A Protest from Paradise," 30; "A Turn in the Sun," 26–28; "The Young Writer's Real Friends," 31
Korean War, 2

Lawrence, D. H., 33
Lewis, R. W. B.: *The American Adam*, 111

major characters in *A Separate Peace*:
Finny (Phineas): attitude toward war, 83, 87–88, 99; compared to Christ, 86; compared to Gabriel Oak, 47; compared to Holden Caulfield, 15; compared to Huckleberry Finn, 99; compared to Lazarus, 56, 86; death, 103, 106–7; disregard of rules, 47, 49, 50, 51, 53, 54, 57, 64; fall from tree, 60–61; fall down stairwell, 102; Super Suicide Society, 24, 51–52, 59, 60; love of singing, 24, 98–99; mythic aspects, 88–90; physical description, 43, 44, 55, 76, 115–16; pink shirt, 24, 47–48, 49, 70; religious beliefs, 23; skill at sports, 7, 24, 43, 44, 52–53, 54, 76, 95–96, 97, 106; stages Winter Carnival, 88–90; theory that war is a hoax, 83, 97, 99, 105
Forrester, Gene: as Finny's double, 63–66; as intellectual, 10, 58, 64; as narrator, 10, 34–40; 41–42; 68, 90; assumes Finny's traits, 75, 78, 84, 109; attitude toward war and military, 8, 51, 80–81, 82–83, 85, 88, 93, 98, 99, 105, 107, 108–9, 110–11; compared to ancient mariner, 60; compared to Judas, 77, 84, 86; compared to Lt. Frederic Henry, 74; compared to Mersault in Camus' *The Stranger*, 60; confessions of guilt, 71–73, 103–6; confused sense of identity, 93, 104, 106; feelings of anxiety, 34–35, 37, 41; fight with Quackenbush, 75–76; forgiven by Finny, 103–6; guilty conscience, 25–26, 38, 71, 72, 78–79, 93, 104; on trial, 78–79; 100–102, 104; physical description, 43, 44, 55; regeneration, 81, 96; rivalry with Finny, 43, 44, 45, 59, 68; sarcastic tone of, 32, 37, 42; suspicion of Finny, 43, 44, 54–57, 59, 60–70, 106; treachery to Finny, 25, 60; trip to Vermont, 90–94; wears Finny's clothes, 70–71

Index

About the Author

Hallman Bryant is director of graduate studies and professor of English at Clemson University in Clemson, South Carolina, where he teaches courses in nineteenth century British literature. He is the author of a book about Robert Graves and has written scholarly essays and reviews of Victorian and modern American literature.